THE SCENT OF ROSEWATER

The SCENT OF ROSEWATER

A NEW ZEALAND BRIDE IN IRAN

ANNA WOODWARD SWINBURN

SHOAL BAY PRESS

DEDICATION

To Mamajan, who taught Anna
what it meant to be a woman in Iran.

First published in 1998 by
Shoal Bay Press Ltd
Box 17-661, Christchurch

Copyright © 1998 Mary D. Woodward

ISBN 0 908704 75 5

All rights reserved. No part of this publication may be reproduced, stored in a retrieval system or transmitted in any form by any means electronic, mechanical, photocopying, recording or otherwise, without prior permission from the publisher.

Cover design by Sarah Maxey

Printed by Rainbow Print Ltd, Christchurch

CONTENTS

	Prologue	7
1	My Arrival in Iran	9
2	Introduction to the Family	13
3	Exploring Tehran	19
4	An Iranian Wedding	27
5	North to the Caspian Sea	33
6	A Chilling Encounter	39
7	My New Home	44
8	Ghosts from the Past	50
9	Mashad, the Holy City	56
10	Learning to Fit In	62
11	Out and About	69
12	A Country at War	82
13	Finding a Husband for Soraya	87
14	Can I Survive Here?	91
15	Golsara, Place of Flowers	99
16	A Visit to the Academy of Beauty	109
17	Our Wedding	111
18	The Ambassador Entertains	121
19	Honeymoon in Isfahan	125
20	In and Around Mashad	129
21	High Summer	137
22	Taher Abad	142
23	The Decision to Leave Iran	148
24	Shiraz and Persepolis	151
25	'Crime' and Punishment	158
26	Farewell to Iran	162
	Epilogue	169
	Chapter Notes	173
	Acknowledgments	176

PROLOGUE

I am Anna's mother, and today is 1 September 1983. It is a sad day for me, for I have just returned from the airport where I put her on a plane and I don't know when I shall see her again. At this very moment she is winging her way towards Iran – of all places on earth the one to be avoided at this time: a country still reeling from a bloody and violent revolution and now engaged in a ferocious war with its long-term enemy, Iraq; a country that is often featured in the news on television, with its thousands of bodies bent in prayer, its angry attacks on the West, and its new leader, Ayatollah Khomeyni, invoking the people in strongly emotive language to return to a way of life guided by fundamental Islamic tenets.

Anna is 26. After losing her teenage puppy fat and braces, cutting off her plaits and exchanging her glasses for contact lenses that make her eyes appear even larger and more luminous, she blossomed from an ugly duckling into a most beautiful and graceful swan. There are lots of pleasant young men of our acquaintance training to be doctors or architects or engineers. Why couldn't she have settled down with one of them, bought a house in Auckland, and given me a clutch of grandchildren, as all my friends' daughters seem to be doing? Why did she have to fall in love with an Iranian?

I was with her when she met Bijan, in England in 1978, and from their first mutual glance I had a premonition that some strange twist of fate was going to bind our three lives together.

I love Bijan. I got to know him well when he followed Anna back to Auckland and they set up house in a tiny flat in Mount Eden, a happy threesome with Azizam, the beloved black cat. Each weekend they would come out to Titirangi where I was living with my young son Paul, and the sad echoes in that house that felt so empty and silent would be driven out by laughter, music and companionship.

But the day came when Bijan confessed that he must follow his heart and return to Iran to see his parents, after years of being parted from them over the hard times of the revolution and the difficult years that followed. In Iran the family – the clan, the tribe – is perhaps more important than it is in our culture so we understood his need and supported him in his decision. What we weren't to know was that on the very day he flew away the war between Iran and Iraq would explode, and once he had set foot in his own country he would be trapped. His passport was removed, for all young men between the ages of 15 and 30 were forbidden to leave in case they were needed for the war.

The two young people tried to forget each other but could not. Bijan planned an escape but was caught and thrown into prison. Another attempt would have been fatal. So the only option was for Anna to go to him. She applied for a visa, and for two long years I secretly prayed that it would be refused. But at last it came, and I had to hide my fears and rejoice with her while we planned their reunion.

But this is her story and I must let her tell it.

CHAPTER 1

MY ARRIVAL IN IRAN

We were flying over Iran, on the last leg of the flight. I felt suffocated with excitement mixed with apprehension as I looked down from the aircraft, my eyes drawn with morbid fascination across that never-changing landscape of jagged mountains like scabs on the barren plains that spread out in all directions. The earth seemed tortured in its desolation except for the occasional tiny patch of green, lush and vivid against the bleached colourlessness of its surroundings. A road – or was it a pipeline? – was etched across the desert as far as the eye could see, in a precise unwavering line.

I had been seated next to the only other European on the flight, an English engineer. At one stage I had turned to him for moral support but he was little help, saying brusquely, 'I go to Iran on business only when I am forced to. And get out as soon as the job is done.'

Thus rebuffed I sat in silence with my thoughts. Thoughts of Bijan, the man who had enchanted me and welcomed me into his world. A beautiful gracious foreigner who wanted me as his partner in life.

'Will you be there to meet me?' I had asked him anxiously during a phone call, for I knew that his home city, Mashad, was far from the capital where we would be landing.

'I will be there with flowers,' he had replied calmly. 'Let me use an old Persian saying to express how I feel. You mean as much to me as my eyes.'

Sitting apparently calm and poised next to the Englishman, I was inwardly a battleground of emotions. The storm of questions, anxieties and fears planted by others and echoed in my own nightmares; the peace of trusting, the acceptance and exhilaration at the heart of the adventure. I was entering the forbidden land, which had tried for many months to keep me out. Like those ancestors who had pioneered my own young country I was committing myself to the unknown. It felt like madness – like stepping off a cliff into the dark, in the face of all warnings. But at the very centre of my being stillness reigned, and the certainty that this was where I was meant to be at this moment of my life.

Of course the easy way out would have been simply to forget him, and this is what my friends and family had urged me to do. Even Iran's portly representative in New Zealand had flinched when I told him of my determination to visit his troubled land.[1] He nodded and bowed and wished me good luck – but did absolutely nothing to help me get a visa. During the few days I had spent in Bahrain en route with Trilby and Ahmed, my old friends from England, I had felt like a monkey in a circus as an endless stream of friends and relatives came by the house to see me for themselves and hear of my crazy plan. American magazines were produced with articles showing women swathed in chadours[2] glaring from the pages, and limousines full of gun-toting mullahs in dark glasses, looking like figures from the Chicago underworld. Horror stories and lists of atrocities were related endlessly.

But despite them all I was nearly there. A tug on my arm brought my reverie to an end. A stewardess leaned towards me, carefully avoiding the sleeping engineer. 'Please cover your hair, madam, we are about to land in Tehran.'

Bijan had emphasised several times in his letters that when I disembarked I must be covered from head to foot. I felt colourless and anonymous in my long black coat and thick stockings, with a scarf hiding my hair. No make-up, no nail polish, no perfume. Like an actor dressed for the part.

I tucked every last strand of hair out of sight as the mammoth expanse of Tehran came into view, spreading funnel-like from the base of the towering Alborz mountains into the desert plains beyond.

There was no doubt about where we had touched down. Ayatollah Khomeyni's bearded face, the stern eyes under heavy arched eyebrows that seemed raised in judgment, looked down from every wall. His green-clad guards also watched, and seemed to judge, standing at their posts with weapons at their sides, their faces grave. Passengers who had glanced warmly in my direction on the plane now lowered their eyes. There were no smiles here; life was obviously a grim business.

Hard-faced customs officers removed and examined every single object in my luggage, constantly throwing me questioning glances, as if wishing to catch me out. Hearing that tampons were unavailable in Iran, I had tucked in dozens of them wherever there was a space, and these were examined with smirks of distaste. (I did not know then that in Muslim societies a woman is considered unclean during menstruation.) Like a timid child, always half prepared to be found at fault by an over-zealous parent, I became nervous. But my thorough preparations paid off, for they found nothing illegal, nothing forbidden by Islamic law. Soon a porter was pushing my trolley towards the arrival hall.

And then I saw him. His dark head and smiling eyes. The long years of waiting were over.

I was engulfed in a wave of flowers and hugs as strange women in flowing chadours chattering at me unintelligibly took my arms and led me out into the dusk. As we got into the car Bijan touched me for the first time, a quick brushing of lip to cheek, and whispered, 'I cannot touch you in public.'

Into the notorious Tehran traffic we swept. I vaguely noticed a huge tower standing on four giant legs at a wide roundabout. 'Freedom Square,' said Bijan. We passed many partly constructed concrete buildings – everything modern, nothing of the ancient here.

Did we talk? I don't remember. Holding and squeezing hands, catching each other's eyes in the rear mirror, aware of the giggling children crammed into the back seat with Bijan's mother, we left the turmoil of the city and headed towards the mountains, dark and looming so near in the fading light. We finally drew up outside a brightly lit house belonging to Bijan's sister.

Once inside, Bijan wrapped me in his arms and nestled his head on my shoulder. I felt a huge sigh release in his body. His dark eyes shimmered, lit with a smile and with tears, as we breathed together and whispered. The moment of relief and rediscovery stretched over us, holding us in its joy. Our journeying had brought us home at last.

CHAPTER 2

INTRODUCTION TO THE FAMILY

As I had been shown to my bedroom shortly after my late arrival in Tehran, it was not until breakfast the next morning that I was properly introduced to all the members of the family who lived in Tehran and those who had come to meet me from Mashad.

We sat on cushions around the sofreh, a cloth spread on the floor, with the food before us and the samovar[3] boiling noisily at the side.

'Look,' said Bijan, 'this is how you do it.' He showed me how to suck up the weak black tea through a sugar cube held in the mouth, and how to make tasty mouthfuls from the unleavened bread wrapped around carrot jam and clotted cream, or goat's milk cheese, fresh mint and walnuts.

His mother, Mamajan (dear mother), sat next to me and we each surreptitiously eyed the other. I sensed her strength and guessed that the entire family revolved around this woman. She had beautiful eyes, a strong proud nose, and the sturdy constitution of a survivor. Her way of welcoming me was by plying me with food, speaking to me in Farsi as she did so. I nodded and smiled, though I did not understand a word she said. Bijan did not translate her words to me, obviously deciding to leave us to work it out between us. Though we did not speak the same language a bond began to be formed.

Also seated with us were Bijan's two married sisters, Nadia and Parvaneh, with their husbands, Daniel and Ibrahim, and Bijan's youngest sister, Soraya, who, though little more than a schoolgirl, had the best grasp of English. There were several children from three to 13, whose names would soon be familiar to me. The children, so beautiful with their coffee-cream skin and dark eyes, were dying to touch me and would approach me and gently stroke my hair, darting a mischievous look at me, then run away triumphantly. Though the adults' welcome could hardly have been warmer, there was nevertheless a slight reticence towards this stranger in their midst. But the children took me to their hearts without reserve.

Taking my hand they showed me around the huge house, first the ballroom, a great cavern with marble pillars reaching up to the ceiling two storeys above, its carpets rolled up and pushed against the walls, the ornate period furniture draped and shrouded in dust sheets. It was a room in mourning for those happy party days Bijan had described to me when its doors were flung open onto the courtyard, and musicians played their traditional instruments and sang, heads thrown back, voices quavering and shimmying.

I drew back some heavy brocade drapes and looked out onto a wildly overgrown garden and marble patio littered with leaves. Beyond was a swimming pool, empty except for a few inches of green slime in the bottom. No more parties, no more music, no more dancing, no more swimming where one could be overlooked by neighbours: all these activities were now strongly discouraged. In another room the children pulled back a heavy curtain revealing, unexpectedly, a huge mosaic of gallant youths and doe-eyed women in voluptuous postures, drinking wine poured from decorated jars. Omar Khayyam's Persia, but covered, smothered.

Below ground, the basement was empty, and the servants' quarters long out of use. The grand house was slowly decaying, largely unused, unfinished, unsaleable, in a suburb of other unused, unfinished, unsaleable mansions. Who wanted to invest in property in a country at war? Who wanted to live in a nouveau riche suburb in those angry times?

I was musing on these observations with Soraya when Bijan made a shock announcement: 'We have to get married today. We'll go to the mosque later this morning where a mullah will perform the ceremony.'

'Married?' I hadn't imagined things would move quite so fast!

'Yes, married temporarily, so that we can be together as man and wife. We must be married to go anywhere in public without a chaperone.'

He explained that Islam recognised two kinds of marriage. The temporary marriage, sigheh, could last for anything from one night to six months, and could be terminated at any time. The permanent marriage, aroosi, involved a lifetime commitment that rarely ended in divorce.

I remembered Ahmed telling me that his father led a yearly hajj, the Muslim pilgrimage to Mecca where the prophet Muhammad is buried. Prior to departure he 'married' all the women whom he would be accompanying, often up to 100. Should he inadvertently touch one of them or see her without her hair covered, he was protected from sin by the act of sigheh. The Islamic code, Shariah, forbade a Muslim to be alone in the company of a member of the opposite sex who was not a spouse or close relative. A woman must be covered from head to foot, even in her own home, whenever there was an unrelated man present.

'The pasdaran, the Revolutionary Guards, patrol the streets in great numbers,' explained Bijan, 'and if you are caught ignoring any of the strict rules of conduct, they will harass you and make life very unpleasant. In some cases it could even lead to slashing.'

Slashing? I needed no further convincing.

Mamajan gave me one of her chadours to wear. She showed me how to pull it forwards, covering my hair entirely, then tuck it back over my mouth. Our eyes met as we walked together to the car, thus enshrouded, and we smiled. She was to be my mentor, teaching what it meant to be a woman in this society. I felt anonymous in my chadour but I did not mind. It was fun to dress up like a Muslim, and anyway gave me the opportunity better to observe the place to which I had come, as from behind a screen.

Daniel and Mamajan were to accompany us; these two very devout Muslims would add weight to our request for sigheh, for Bijan did not practise the outward formalities of his faith. Daniel's professional standing as a leading plastic surgeon could also prove to be an asset.

This time, as we drove away from the house, I was able to take in more of my surroundings. The land in the neighbourhood of Parvaneh's home was, at the time of the revolution five years earlier, being developed as a new and wealthy suburb. Perched on the foothills of the Alborz mountains were hundreds of ambitious mansions, many of them standing gaunt and unfinished on their treeless plots, deserted by owners who had fled abroad, and now sometimes taken over by the very servants who had reported their masters' 'sins' to the authorities. The homes were built in European style without high walls cutting them off from the street, which was in nearly every case badly potholed and neglected.

Daniel explained, in his sketchy English, that because this was a wealthy area, like all the suburbs in the north of Tehran on the mountain slopes, it was among the first to be deprived of power, water and maintenance services, all of which were in short supply. The southern part of the city where the poor in their millions struggled to live was now, since the revolution, favoured with attention from the government. The revolution championed the underdog and the wealthy were to be humbled, for many of them had profited through their association with the regime of the deposed Shah.

He told me that Parvaneh and Ibrahim had built their ambitious marble-faced home with borrowed money as an investment, their aim being to sell it to the Argentinean government as a diplomatic residence. But the revolution had put an end to their plans. There were now too many such houses and few takers.

Against the skyline stood huge concrete skeletons surrounded by rusting cranes and scaffolding. Many a dream of cashing in on the attraction Iran used to hold for foreign investment was crumbling to dust with those petrified shapes.

The traffic became more hectic and the streets uglier as we descended into the heart of Tehran. Homes and gardens were no longer visible from the streets, being tucked behind high concrete walls, many of which were decorated with graffiti and violent murals carrying the message of hatred for the Shah and for Iran's enemies. Mercifully, the main avenues were lined with autumn-tinged poplars, which brought some life and shade to an otherwise dun-coloured city.

The small mosque near which we parked was not the glorious domed specimen I had imagined. It was a concrete building, squat and unattractive but for the elaborate mosaic work edging the arched entrance. The interior was gloomy, but spacious and tranquil. We slipped off our shoes just inside the entrance and walked in stockinged feet over the worn Persian carpets

Anna at three.

Anna aged four or five, dancing.

Anna with her pony Nell.

From 'ugly duckling' to 'swan'.

Anna and Galushka.

Anna and Bijan in Derby.

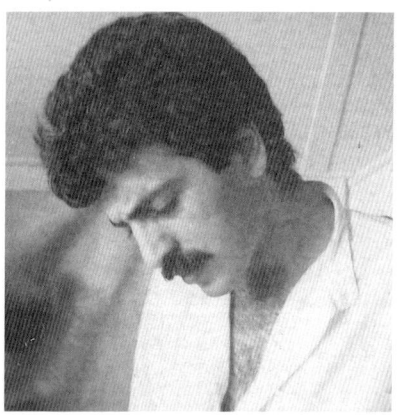

Bijan. 'I thought he was the most beautiful man in the world.'

Anna and Trilby in Bahrein.

A deserted palace, Bahrein.

Standing by another ruin in Bahrein.

Trilby and Ahmed entertain

A corner of our apartment where 'every prospect pleases'.

Bijan bringing home the bread

that lined the large open space. Several figures were tucked to the floor, like neat mounds, in prayer. We sat in silence at a small wooden table in one corner of the mosque, and a turbaned mullah soon joined us. I had no idea what to expect; nor, I realised, did my companions for whom this was also a new experience.

Sitting opposite me, the mullah began to address me in a quiet voice, looking down at the table between us. He did not at any point raise his eyes to look into my face. Bijan translated what he said.

'He asks if you wish to adopt the Islamic faith.'

I nodded and said, 'Bale'.

'How many gods are there?'

'One god,' I replied.

'Who was Jesus Christ?'

'One of the prophets like Muhammad.' I knew that this was the way Muslims thought of Jesus. He was revered as a messenger from Allah, as was Muhammad who came after him. Thus, according to Muslims, Islam was a natural progression from Christianity. I also considered Jesus in this way.

The mullah nodded approvingly.

'Repeat this koranic prayer after me. Bismillah raman o raheem …'

He intoned the prayer, full of guttural Arabic sounds that I did my best to imitate. I did not know the meaning of what I said. The long prayer finished, the mullah spoke to Bijan for several minutes.

'Do you like the name Zahra?' Bijan asked me. 'It's a very good Muslim name, the name of Muhammad's daughter. We need to find a Muslim name for you.' So Zahra I became (but only on paper), to the nodding approval of Daniel and Mamajan.

His duties completed, the mullah rose to leave us, his downturned eyes glowing. He seemed to regard my 'conversion' to Islam as a personal victory.

We had been granted six months' sigheh, but I felt uncomfortable that no documentary evidence had been provided to prove it. This seemed strange in a country where I believed identity papers would surely be necessary.

'I asked him for a document but he said it was not necessary,' said Bijan. 'He said that if we are questioned we must refer the Revolutionary Guards directly to him.'

So Bijan wrote down the mullah's name and the location of the mosque as we drove away, this time sitting side by side in the back of the car, man and (temporary) wife.

CHAPTER 3

EXPLORING TEHRAN

The whole household now seemed enlivened and excited, reflecting the joy we two felt at being allowed to be together in total intimacy. Yesterday what was punishable by slashing had now become, with the sanction of the mullah, a cause for celebration. While we were away at the mosque Nadia and Parvaneh had been shopping for flowers and had decorated the room we were to occupy with a towering vase of gladioli and a low bowl of tumbling roses. There were bowls of pistachios, and a cornucopia of fruit. The linen of the vast bed – made up of two beds pushed together – had been liberally sprinkled with rosewater while cassettes of Iranian music had been placed to hand beside the tape recorder. In later years, whenever I heard the exquisite voice of Pari Zanganeh, memories of that special time came flooding back, and I would find myself smiling.

Safe now to be alone together, Bijan and I spent much of the next week exploring the vast city of Tehran. He knew it well, having spent a year there when he was younger, using the period of exemption from military service to explore career options before going to England to complete the language qualification necessary for tertiary education in that country.

I learned later from Mamajan that Bijan had become a bit of a problem in his late teens. Although bright, he had not been interested in academic subjects. He had excelled in sport – in swimming, athletics and basketball – for he was tall and strong and very quick on his feet. But having gone as far as he could in school sports, captaining the various teams, he had become bored and hard to live with. So he was packed off to stay with his sister in Tehran.

Bijan was thrilled by this wonderful city, its extraordinary wealth and sophistication equal to those of any other.

There his real talents started to emerge. He discovered that he could sell almost anything, and was soon engaged in wheeling and dealing, mostly cars. He was also a shrewd gambler, and played poker far into the night with the many wealthy contacts he made through family and friends. So he found himself always with money in his pocket, and went each day to the barber to be shaved and have his moustache trimmed.

He developed a taste for fine clothes and dressed in the latest gear. Around him gathered a circle of young men who looked to him as the leader, such was his charisma. It was not hard to imagine him having a great year in Tehran! But when I remarked that his description of Tehran made it sound like a Middle Eastern Las Vegas Bijan objected strongly, for along with the fashionable restaurants, luxury hotels and a nightlife that never slept, the city boasted several top-ranking universities, great opera houses, concert halls and theatres, and was on the circuit for all world-famous artists. But at the age of 18 Bijan had definitely been attracted to the city's less cultural attributes.

Tehran now was home to about 10 million people. Bijan told me how, since the early 1970s, many peasants had left the villages where their families had lived for generations. They sought to avoid the hardships resulting from the Shah's rural policies, but found only greater difficulties to be overcome in the overcrowded city. Refugees from the war zones, as well as many 'Afghani visitors' who sought refuge from the political problems in their own country, contributed to the stress.

Where we were staying in the north of the city it was easy to remain unaware of the problems of the mass of humanity struggling to survive in the south. Each year, in earlier days, wealthy families were able to retreat to their palatial summer quarters on the mountain slopes, for relief from the heat of the desert plains. Eventually the large holdings were subdivided and permanent suburbs of luxurious houses in pleasant gardens on leafy streets were created. It was the place to live if you could choose.

We walked up steep mountain paths beside waterfalls, looking above our heads to magnificent homes tucked away in privacy on their exclusive ledges. Tiny cafés served tea and delicate sweets. Many of these were accessible only on foot over wooden bridges spanning the rapids, with terraces hanging over the fast-flowing river. Old men stood beside the winding paths selling freshly shelled walnuts, which they fished out of enormous glass jars full of salted water.

We shopped in the once-elegant arcades, which were inspired in their elaborate decor by European influences. The plush boutiques were attended by women who could not wear the imported clothing they were trying to sell. Yet somehow they managed to look elegant in the only acceptable alternative to the chadour, the long coat and headscarf.

As soon as I was recognised as a foreigner, I received special attention and was shown the most expensive goods. Obviously foreign women married only very wealthy Iranian men!

In their broken English, the shop assistants told me of the 'good old days' of the Shah, when Tehran was the Paris of the Middle East. Designer fashions from the top European houses were often available here before they were to be found in Europe. Looking at the prices, I realised that there must still be great wealth in this city. But where would the women wear all this jewellery and clothing for which they had paid a fortune? Bijan assured me that for private social functions the women dressed like fashion plates.

We dined on the famous Persian caviar and sturgeon at the last of the fine restaurants. Service was gracious and attentive, to the sound of tasteful chamber music, the only form of music permissible. (Popular music is regarded as a distraction to religion, and modern Western music in general a corrupting influence.) The food was beautifully presented, and I appreciated the fresh flowers on each table. This was a gracious touch that may have been considered frivolous in restaurants more accessible to the general public, for whom the revolution took precedence over everything else in life.

I have to confess that it did feel strange to be offered Coca-Cola to accompany the superb food, instead of a bottle of white wine. The atmosphere was very subdued, with most people speaking in hushed, conspiratorial tones. No laughter, no gaiety. All this, I was to discover, was not due to polite manners, but more to the fact that these people had been accustomed to being watched and listened to for many years now by the Shah's secret police, Savak,[4] and were wary of communicating in public. And now there could be others listening.

Gracious living was still possible in Tehran, if one could overlook the power cuts and potholes, but you needed plenty of money.

Descending from the mountainside suburbs, we drove down poplar-lined avenues, our ears filled with the sound of gushing water flowing in the deep roadside channels, towards the commercial centre and the slums in the south of Tehran. Here the effects of the revolution and the signs of a country at war were impossible to ignore. Limbless soldiers swinging along on crutches, wheelchairs in shop windows alongside walls of photos of the martyrs, such intense young faces. Many shrines decorated with lights or flowers took up space on the footpath, commemorating the martyr whose photo was displayed. The streets were crowded and dusty, with beggars at their favourite stations, bearded government employees in crumpled suits hurrying about their work, chadoured women clutching children and baskets weaving their way unobtrusively through the knots of gossiping businessmen, manual workers digging up streets and laying pipes, delivery men bent under their loads. Launching oneself into the crazy traffic in order to cross a street was a major hazard.

Tehran's bazaar, the most extensive in Asia, spilled out onto the street near the huge Friday mosque, so called because it housed the services on the holy day, Friday. When I asked Bijan if this mosque was the background in all those shots of praying bodies moving in unison that we had seen so often on television, he explained that those pictures had been taken in the grounds of Tehran University. I wondered then whether a mosque was forbidden territory for cameras. There was so much I wanted to know – needed to know – but I held my tongue, realising much would become clear in time.

In several of the public squares Bijan pointed out empty pedestals that had recently carried statues of the Shah or his father, Reza Shah, founder of the Pahlavi dynasty. They had all been dismantled. Every reminder of Iran's imperial past was to be blotted out. Pages bearing pictures of the Shah or his family had been torn out of books for sale in bookshops. Sometimes the figures had been blacked out.

On a visit to one of the Shah's palaces we were made painfully aware of the extravagant opulence of the carpets, furniture and table settings. They stood, in stark contrast, next to huge photographs of suffering people that had been placed judiciously to make a point. The only reminder of the family that had lived there, apart from the unbelievable contents of the wardrobes, was one large photograph of His Imperial Majesty – upside down!

In the carpet museum we watched a Persian carpet being made by hand, and marvelled at the variety of patterns, the glowing colours and the extreme intricacy of many of the hundreds of carpets on show.

My Bahraini friend Ahmed was right: beauty did still live here, though it had often been abandoned in the struggle for survival.

Bijan and I talked for hours about the years we had been apart, sharing all the feelings that letters could never contain. We lay together in silence trying to come to terms with his troubled country, his torn culture and his weary family, and I began to understand him so much more, and felt a deep compassion, particularly for his mother and sisters. I began to appreciate their reticence towards me. They had all been through so much that a stranger could never be expected to understand or share.

Bijan told me about his attempt to escape. He and a friend had planned it many months ahead and had arranged a Baluchi guide to take them over the mountains. But just as they were boarding a bus in Zahidan that would take them to a remote village, pasdaran (Revolutionary Guards) appeared and asked for papers. I said he had probably drawn attention to himself because, always an impeccable dresser, he had looked too clean and well groomed to be a Baluchi peasant!

He had been questioned and arrested, but not before he had unobtrusively passed over to his friend the money he had on him. The bus had drawn away with his friend on board, but whether he had ever reached safety Bijan did not know. For several weeks Bijan languished in jail in Zahidan, never knowing if or when he would be put before the firing squad. Then one day he was simply released without explanation, but with a strong warning against trying to escape again. Waiting at the prison gates he found his parents and cousin, who was a general practitioner in Zahidan. They had made representations to the authorities, who had then ascertained that Bijan was not a member of the Mujaheddin, opposed to the government, and was not primarily trying to escape conscription. He was simply trying to get back to his fiancée.

I remembered well the anxiety of that time, and the difficulty of communication between us. It was suspected that phone lines were being tapped, and some letters arrived having been opened. But somehow without it being spelled out I got a hint that he was planning to make a dash for freedom into Pakistan, where my Uncle John was heading a United Nations mission in charge of a camp of three-quarters of a million Afghani refugees in the mountainous region of Quetta. What a blessing that Bijan's escape bid failed, for John told me later on his return to New Zealand that Revolutionary Guards from Iran were patrolling the border between Iran and Pakistan and sometimes shooting refugees on sight. At times John had had the opportunity to save some of them by placing them in the security of a lock-up until arrangements could be made to 'lose' them in one of the teeming cities of India.

The time in Tehran also gave me the opportunity to get to know a little about those members of the family who had travelled so far to greet me.

Bijan's sister Nadia, the eldest, was a tall, well-built woman with short black hair and soft, luminous eyes. She had trained as a paediatrician and managed a busy practice. I could imagine that she would inspire confidence in her patients with her warmth, her calm manner and her practical common sense. Already it felt as if she was beginning to emulate her mother's role as matriarch of a large, successful family, for she seemed to make all the decisions. Her husband, Daniel, had done his post-graduate training in plastic surgery in Germany. He understood and spoke basic English, though with some amusing oddities, such as using the definite article before proper nouns, for example, 'the Tehran'. And I always had to hide my smile when he spoke of 'the revelation'. He was a strict Muslim, who never failed in his observances, and who impressed me immediately as a man of great integrity, though he lacked the gentleness of Bijan. I picked that he would be a loving but strict father.

Soon after my arrival Nadia and Daniel returned to their home and work in Mashad, leaving a more peaceful house and the opportunity for closer relationships.

Soraya, a highly intelligent 18-year-old and a real beauty with her slim figure and cascading black hair, spoke of her frustration at having to mark time learning embroidery instead of studying medicine as she would have been doing, had the universities not been closed. She soon began to follow me around with admiring eyes, and we developed a close friendship for there were only seven years between us. With me she could relax and laugh at some of the excesses of Islamic life, though she was still very devout in her practices.

Bijan had often spoken of Parvaneh, aptly translated as Butterfly. She was the fun-loving, popular sister who shone at parties and was the best dancer. She had always dressed with style and had the money to do so. But Parvaneh was now exhausted with the work of running the huge home without help, and managing on a stringent budget after many carefree years. Above all, however, she was crushed by the fear that her young son would be unable to escape being sent as cannon fodder to the front in a few years' time. The war with Iraq was dragging on with no sign of a resolution. This was a common fear in the family, for Bijan had several nephews in their early teens who would soon be eligible for military service.

We stayed up many nights, sitting on a Persian carpet on the floor of the ballroom while Ibrahim played his mournful santour, softly striking the strings as he spoke about the past.

This small, fiery man had loved his work in the computer industry and been very successful. But he had become discouraged by what he saw as a move against modernisation at a national level, and feared for his prosperity under the new regime. He had decided to change direction and became a producer of baby food, figuring that there would always be babies!

Ibrahim spoke English well as he had spent time in the United States. He enjoyed practising his English on me and was hungry to talk.

'Oh, if only I could describe to you how Iran used to be in the days when life was easy; if only you had come here then!' He talked of the wealth and the opportunities, and of the way the country had started to adapt to what he considered valuable changes, changes that had been brought about by the opening up of Iran to the wider world.

'Iran had everything: money, style, a proud history and an ancient culture, as well as all the modern conveniences. Iran was certainly on the map then and we Iranians were welcome all over the world because we brought money with us. Our luck has run out again. We are back where we started. Such waste.'

I was to hear the same story over and over again in the ensuing months.

CHAPTER 4

AN IRANIAN WEDDING

It was a lucky coincidence that a wedding in the family of Parvaneh's in-laws was to take place during the time Bijan and I were in Tehran. So, being temporarily part of her household, we were invited to attend. Everyone took an afternoon nap and then busied themselves getting ready to make an appearance at the wedding in the early evening. The women had touched up the grey in their dark hair, and donned chic dresses, plenty of fine jewellery and beautiful handmade shoes, all to be hidden under the dark chadours during the trip in the car.

On the way to the wedding I was told something of the young people who were to be married. They had been introduced four months earlier by the girl's parents, who had been looking for a suitable husband for their 18-year-old daughter, Nilofar (Waterlily). When Hossein, a 33-year-old civil engineer, had approached them, having heard of Nilofar from relatives, they had made enquiries, and only after making sure that he had a suitable background and a good reputation did they allow the couple to meet. Over the following two months Nilofar and Hossein got to know each other, meeting once a week in Nilofar's home, diligently chaperoned. They liked each other, so planned to marry within another two months.

Where, I wondered, was the passion in all this? Where was love? In my world you married for love, not because you *liked* the other person! I remembered my own unforgettable meeting with Bijan at a party in England, how we caught sight of each other at the same moment, 'across a crowded room', and the magic began to work.

I had been travelling in England with my parents at the time and we had decided to visit my childhood friend Trilby, who was living in Derby. The house, one of those narrow ones with about five storeys, was owned by a charming woman called Gail, or Galushka as everyone called her. She had gathered about herself a group of young people who shared the house with her. All Galushka's friends had to be 'interesting' in some ill-defined way: stunningly beautiful, or witty, or full of anecdotes from a colourful past, or simply outrageous.

Galushka opened the door to us, dressed in jodhpurs, high boots and a silk shirt open almost to the waist. She was very slim with a chic haircut. She must have thought we looked sufficiently 'interesting' because she promptly invited us to a party there that night. (I was to learn that there was a party at Galushka's every night!) We duly arrived at the appointed hour and were shown into a crowded drawing-room full of smoke and chatter. I looked across the room and saw this tall figure half turned away, and at that very moment he turned and our eyes met. I felt a sort of shock and in that moment knew that this man had some part to play in my destiny.

Later as we sat in Bijan's room at the top of the house, he confessed that he had experienced the same sensation. And I began to realise that he was very different from the young men I had grown up with.

On the walls of his room were pinned up beautiful prints from many cultures. A very long silk scarf hung from the rafters and was pinned back to reveal its glowing colours. On his bed a handwoven coverlet was thrown, and the tapes he put into his cassette player were of a great variety of musical styles. He showed me his favourite books, some of poetry, others containing amazing photographs. He seemed to have no concept that such interests might be considered unmanly, as would often have been the case back in the New Zealand of the 1970s. He was not afraid of being gentle, of revealing his feelings. I began to fall in love with him, and that night I didn't leave his room at the top of the house. As we drove to the wedding listening to the talk of arranged marriages, Bijan squeezed my hand and I knew he too was remembering.

By the time we arrived at the home of the bride, where the wedding was to take place, many guests were already seated in large rooms lined around the walls with chairs. In one room all the women were gathered, obviously enjoying the opportunity to have a good gossip with friends and relatives, and for those who had discarded their chadour on arrival, to show off their clothes, jewels and hairstyles. By contrast, the men in the next room, looking awkward in their suits, sat in stiff silence, with little to do except drink endless cups of tea and eat little cakes. They had obviously accompanied their wives more out of a sense of duty than the prospect of a good time.

After several cups of tea and many introductions, I was taken to view the specially arranged room where the ceremony would take place.

Photographers were busy setting up lights and cameras, focusing on a low stool next to a large white satin sheet. This was spread on the floor and a number of objects symbolising the good life had been placed on it: a silver framed mirror and matching pair of candlesticks; a copy of the Koran wrapped in a finely embroidered cloth; a golden bowl of honey and a little ornamental tree in gold, on which hung the wedding rings; crystal bowls filled with gold-dipped eggs, almonds and walnuts; crystallised sugar tied in bundles with gold threads. A platter of salad and cheese among others of rich sweets and biscuits seemed somewhat out of place in the company of all these symbols of wealth. Enormous floral arrangements of carnations, gladioli and tuberoses stood around the room, while paper flowers adorned the walls.

Another round of tea and cakes, and word spread swiftly through the crowded rooms that the bride was about to descend. Lights were trained on the stairs and photographers stood at the ready, some aiming still cameras, others armed with video recorders. In a dazzle of light she came into view, moving with coy grace into the decorated room, followed by a jostling stream of cheering and clapping women.

She sat on the low stool and surveyed herself in the mirror. In the beauty salon where she had spent many hours earlier in the day this young girl, who had never worn even a touch of lipstick before, had been dramatically made up, with eyes heavily lined in black and fringed with false eyelashes, and lips matching her painted nails. An intricately beaded head-dress secured the veil in place over an ambitious coiffure. Her fitting gown of white lace was appliquéed with flowers, sequins and pearls. As she spoke in a hushed voice to the friends who surrounded her, she kept glancing at the image in the mirror, as though she could not believe what she saw.

Soon came the mullah in the long brown robe and white turban of Iran's religious men. Forbidden to look upon the women, he entered the room with bowed head and seated himself on the floor beside Nilofar, never once looking up. The noisy guests quietened as he began intoning a prayer.

'Bismillah raman o raheem ... (In the name of Allah, the most compassionate and merciful ...)'

In the absence of the groom, who was not yet allowed in, the mullah asked the bride if she would accept Hossein as her life-long partner. As she sat in silence giving no reply, the women who were gathered around broke their hush and began chanting a simple little song, which Parvaneh, standing next to me, translated as a call to the groom to come quickly and catch his bride.

Again the mullah put the question to the bride; again she kept silent. The women, relishing this game in which the bride was playing hard to get, sang their song with even more gusto.

On the third request the bride consented and her reply was greeted with more cheers, clapping and hollering. Now the women repeated their call for the groom. He made his way through the excited throng and took his place on the stool beside Nilofar. The mullah held up an enormous register for them to sign. Then, his duties completed, he left the room, without a glance to left or right.

Shyly, quietly, the newlyweds sat together while a canopy was raised over their heads, and sugar, symbolising the sweetest thing in life, was sprinkled over it. Meanwhile, green, red and blue threads were being stitched into the fabric of the canopy, as if sewing the lives of the young couple together. Beneath the canopy Nilofar and Hossein were exchanging rings, thick gold diamond-studded bands. Then the groom reached forward and picked up the bowl of honey, dipping his little finger into it and offering it for the bride to lick off. Cheered on by the women standing around, she bit his finger hard as she sucked off the honey, proclaiming her intention to be boss in the home. She then offered him a taste of honey, symbolising her pledge to give her best to him.

Showers of coins and notes were tossed over their heads as they stood to receive their gifts. The groom's sister announced each relative as, one by one, they pushed through the crowd to present a small unwrapped box. From each box she pulled out a piece of jewellery, all of which the bride immediately put on: three necklaces including a triple string of pearls, a watch, several gold bracelets and pairs of earrings and almost more rings than she had fingers!

Throughout the ceremony I had been pushed into a grandstand position, as a newcomer who was expected to be a bride herself before long. What had most impressed me was the enthusiasm with which the 'supporting cast', mainly the female relatives, had prepared and carried out all the symbolic paraphernalia and activities. Obviously they were not disenchanted with marriage as an institution. However, I had been glad to see the bride encouraged to show a little bit of spirit and independence in the finger-biting episode!

After posing for dozens of photographs with the various groups of relatives, the couple promenaded the guest rooms and performed the first dance.

Later in the evening an elaborate feast was laid out. A whole lamb, stuffed with dried fruit and nuts, stood as the centrepiece, surrounded by platters of saffron rice, bowls of chicken in walnut and pomegranate sauce, beef stroganoff and a tangy lamb dish flavoured with lemon and herbs. Salade Olivier, green salads and a selection of pickles made from aubergines, gherkins and other vegetables complemented the meat dishes. There were also bowls of red quince and cherry jams for those with a sweet tooth.

The wedding cake was a layered sponge filled with mock cream flavoured with rosewater, and this, accompanied by fresh fruit, was served as dessert. No wine was served, but copious quantities of the ubiquitous Coke.

This was my first social occasion in Iran and I was interested to see how the men and women, especially the older ones, segregated themselves into different areas of the room. I was introduced to a number of people, and soon realised I had to avoid offering my hand for shaking, which might have proved very embarrassing to a strict Muslim man.

At last, after hours of feasting and dancing, we all departed, leaving the young couple alone for the very first time during the four months of their courtship.

CHAPTER 5

NORTH TO THE CASPIAN SEA

After a week in Tehran Bijan and I left for the trip home to Mashad. Parvaneh blessed our journey, holding up a tray carrying a glass of water and a Koran.[5] We kissed the holy book in turn, then each passed under the tray three times. As we drove off waving she threw the water after the car. This ancient send-off was to ensure a safe return.

There were several routes to Mashad, but Bijan chose the road north over the Alborz Range, part of a broken chain of mountains stretching from the alps of Europe down to the Himalayas. Reaching the Caspian Sea we would head east along the coast to Khorasan, the province in which Mashad was situated.

The road up the mountains was excellent, winding but wide, with many tunnels, wild gorges and bridges spanning deep ravines. On nearly every cliff face revolutionary slogans in blood red paint had been sprayed. Early on we passed a huge dammed lake, which used to be the playground for Tehran's rich. In those days it had a casino and restaurants for entertainment after a day of boating and waterskiing.

Much of the way a river filled the air with the sound of rushing water, its grassy banks dappled with light falling through the golden autumn foliage of the trees. Here and there, high on a mountain slope or deep in a ravine, stood a little mosque, seemingly inaccessible for all but sure-footed goats.

The mountains, rising high on either side of the road, were our companions. At the highest point, where the glorious volcano Mt Damavand towered so near, we stopped for refreshment at a tiny chaikhane,[6] or teahouse, with rickety tables and chairs standing outside in the bitterly cold air. Here I had my first experience of a public toilet in Iran, and I was not impressed!

At regular intervals along the route we encountered a roadblock where grim-faced, uniformed pasdaran searched the car for alcohol, opium or weapons. I was very anxious in case we should be asked for our marriage papers, which of course we did not have, and covered my face as much as possible to prevent the guards from detecting that I was foreign.

Bijan drove fast but hardly spoke. He seemed restless, stopping the car often and pacing the side of the road. I became increasingly concerned but when I asked what was troubling him his answers were curt and noncommital. I began to wonder if I had done something wrong, said something that had angered him. In a strange culture it is so easy to give offence without ever intending to.

As dusk fell we left the mountains behind and drove over flat, fertile land lush with fruit trees and market gardens, land that receives the abundant rainfall prevented from reaching the rest of the country by the wall of mountains. At Ramsar, a small town on the Caspian Sea, we arrived at the house where we were to stay, 10 hours after leaving Tehran.

Then an extraordinary thing happened. As three young men came out of the house at the sound of our horn Bijan suddenly became frantic, calling urgently to the men and lurching out of the car, doubled up with what looked like severe pain. Two of them held him by his arms and bundled him back into his car. One then held him down in the back seat as he writhed in agony, while the other backed down the drive and shot out of sight.

Bijan had told me that three of his closest friends had come over from Mashad to accompany us back, in case we had any trouble, but I had not met them or been aware of a second car waiting discreetly to see that we were not held back at roadblocks. I knew only that their names were Arash, Joseph and Akbar. Now I had been left alone in a strange house in a strange country with a total stranger, who introduced himself as Akbar.

Akbar and I looked at each other. I was utterly bewildered. It was as if Bijan had been holding some incredible pain at bay during the whole long journey from Tehran, and now, as soon as he was with friends he could trust, the whole force of it overwhelmed him.

Akbar tried to explain what had been said, but his language was unintelligible to me and he was no good at mime. He brought me a chair and indicated that I should sit. A small tray with black tea and white sugar cubes was shortly carried in by a middle-aged woman, who was obviously a servant. Akbar sat at some distance from me, protectively but not wanting to intrude. We both knew that further attempts at communication would just make us both more uncomfortable.

The rain started suddenly, heavy sheets pounding on the tin roof, accentuating my sense of isolation. We moved and sat on the verandah and watched it pelting down. We shared the rain and in that sharing began to feel safe with each other.

The time passed. I tried to stay calm, accepting the situation and not fighting it. Akbar offered me a jacket as the night was cool. I looked out over the garden, lush and colourful even in the fading light, with its brilliant greens and sub-tropical reds. This was no garden fed on desert sands.

Finally, two and a half hours after the car had disappeared down the drive, its headlights beamed through the rain. Arash and Joseph emerged and ran for cover. I questioned their unfamiliar faces, feeling a frown on my brow. Arash handed me a small piece of folded paper. His face was serious but otherwise expressionless. My heart beat faster and I opened up the paper with trembling hands.

'Kidney stones. I'm all right. See you in two hours. Love, B.'

Now I understood his agony, for I had heard that kidney stones were among the most painful of ailments. Yet he had not let me know! I was to see this same fortitude in the face of necessity again and again in Bijan, and it never failed to amaze me.

Arash, the group's spokesman, invited me inside out of the cold and we sat in silence. I think they kept silent for fear of offending me by talking together and so excluding me. They waited on me with endless cups of tea and food, and after a short time the vodka came out. Here I was, within a few days of my arrival in this country where alcohol is absolutely forbidden, being offered home-made vodka! People will live the way they choose, against all obstacles.

The appearance of the vodka brought us closer as we exchanged knowing smiles, united in conspiracy against the world out there beyond the gates, the world ordered by fanatics. Indicating that he and Joseph would not drink at this time, as their responsibility still lay with Bijan, Arash poured vodka into a small crystal glass for me. I took my glass of vodka, chilled to a syrupy texture, and sipped it, but my action invited much comment from the men.

'No, no!' they gesticulated. This much vodka was to be drunk in one swig!

They were falling over themselves to make me feel welcome and I did feel in good hands. Arash, in particular, felt as solid as a rock and my instinct was to trust him absolutely. Over the next 18 months, as he became like a brother to me, I came to know that he deserved that trust.

When they finally brought Bijan back, smiling and cheerful, he was high on morphine, but he had passed some stones and the rest were expected to pass by morning. He accepted the vodka that was handed to him and we got down to the serious business of celebrating. It was nearly morning by the time we unpacked the car and headed for bed. What a day!

After a night for me of dreams and nightmares we rose to join the others for breakfast on the verandah. The air was cool and clean and the garden still damp from the rain that had fallen most of the night.

In the morning light I was able to take in more fully our surroundings. The house was modern, quite substantial and comfortable. Without its few Persian ornaments it could have been a beach house in New Zealand. It was the holiday residence of a friend of Joseph's, and was served by the family who lived next door. The garden was therefore well tended and everything kept in good order for the arrival of the owner, and a good meal always available. How different from the unpacking and settling in that had always been part of our family holidays at the beach.

The servants placed warm unleavened bread, each 'loaf' the size and shape of a dinner plate, with cherry jam, fetta cheese and chai, on a cloth on the tiled verandah floor. Invited to join us, the husband and wife sat for a short while and ate modestly. Though the woman had covered her hair, Bijan told me that I need not, as we were on private property. Nevertheless, I was aware that the husband consciously averted his eyes from me, looking ill-at-ease in the presence of an uncovered stranger. However, I was grateful for this small freedom. On the long journey from Tehran, on what really could be called my honeymoon, I had felt a frump in my drab all-enveloping coat, my hair plastered under a black ruhsari.[7] I had yet to discover the knack of making this gear look even moderately attractive.

I asked Bijan if many people still had servants and was told that in the big cities it was very difficult to find people you could trust not to report any breaches of the moral code to the local komiteh.[8] I gathered that this was some sort of panel for controlling un-Islamic behaviour. A servant with a grudge could make life very difficult for her master, and her testimony as a 'good Muslim' would probably carry more weight than his. The lower classes were almost always more orthodox in their religion, not having been exposed to alternatives. So, though Parvaneh in Tehran had to manage without servants, in Mashad, because so many of the family were involved in medical practice and had a number of loyal and grateful patients, trustworthy servants were always available.

From behind the bushes and trees that formed a barrier between this property and the next came the sound of young high voices chanting, and the chanting grew to a great crescendo. I asked Bijan what it was all about. He conferred with the servants briefly before revealing that every morning the little children at the primary school next door were made to chant in unison, 'Death to the United States, death to the Soviet Union, death to Israel!'

To me this form of 'political education' was quite senseless; could this in any way help the children to understand their country's situation in relation to the US, the Soviet Union and Israel? Or would it simply foment a biased hatred in years to come? At this moment, the realisation flooded over me, more strongly than ever before, that I had been so lucky, so blessed, to have been brought up without the need to recognise enemies, without the need to hate.

'But why,' I asked Bijan, 'death to Israel? Haven't Jews lived side by side with Muslims in Iran? Are they not tolerated here like other minority groups, such as the Armenians?'

'You are right. It is not the Jews themselves that Iran hates. It's the aggressive Zionist state of Israel that occupies land that has belonged to Arabs for many centuries, and then refuses to grant them equal rights. You'd think the Jews would have suffered enough racial hatred from the Nazis not to want to inflict it on others. The Palestinians are Arabs, and we are not, but they are our Muslim brothers and we can't forget what has happened to them. The great powers, which after all brought about this situation, don't want to take any responsibility. It's dreadfully unfair.'

It was in a very sober mood that we walked across the rough grassy patch to the deserted beach and the sea, the Caspian Sea, whose shores Iran shared with several republics of the then Soviet Union – Georgia, Kazakstan, Turkmanestan, Azerbaijan – names loaded with mystery for me. I had seen wild Georgian dancers performing, I had read of Samarkand and Bokhara. Now, that world of my fantasies was so near – the very rubbish on the beach had probably washed in from over there. I had grown up in the years of the Cold War so the very word Russia was loaded for me. I looked across that vast stretch of water and wondered about the people who lived there. Did they wonder about me, the way I felt, the way I lived?

Bijan was quite used to having the Soviet Union on his doorstep, for Mashad was not far from the border, and a similar distance from Afghanistan. He had lived his life surrounded by often hostile neighbours, while I had spent mine in the isolation of a lonely ocean, ceaselessly swept by the winds of an uninhabited continent.

I was tempted to swim, although it was cooler here than south of the mountains. But I was told it would not be much fun, as I would have to bathe fully clothed. I could take off my shoes, but that was all. I'd probably have drowned in that ballooning coat!

We laughed then, but did not laugh later when the servants reported that three women had been drowned at a nearby beach that very afternoon, caught in a current and hampered by their chadours.

I was beginning to learn that each day would bring rewards, in the form of love Bijan showered on me and all the new experiences coming my way. But there would also be shocks, and much that was hard to accept.

CHAPTER 6

A CHILLING ENCOUNTER

Next day we packed the cars for the 18-hour journey to Mashad. The men would continue to escort us, at a distance. We drove for hours along the edge of the Caspian, through little seaside towns, their proud but empty hotels waiting for the tourist season, so slack these days that it would hardly ease their struggle to survive; through the rich agricultural provinces of Guilan and Mazandaran, which between them produced as much food as the rest of the country; past clusters of humble dun-coloured homes, their mud-bricks handmade by their inhabitants and sunbaked before being plastered together with a mixture of straw and earth; past ruined villages that were no more than suggestive mounds enclosed by protecting walls built against the invasions of the marauding tribesmen who had swept down from the north over countless centuries. How quickly a thriving settlement, once deserted for whatever reason, crumbled back into the dust from which it had been made, all the drama of the lives that had been lived there vanished entirely.

Like a patchwork around the small settlements were the orchards and vegetable gardens to feed the villagers, while the larger enterprises, such as tea plantations and rice paddies on the hillsides, drew workers from a wider area. There were no 'farmhouses' as we knew them in New Zealand. Everyone evidently lived in the village and worked a small piece of land nearby. It reminded me of the projects we had done as school children on medieval life in Europe.

Our route took us east, where the towns became bigger and busier and the population mixed with a colourful and exotic element with oriental looks and flamboyant dress. Bijan explained that this influence was due to the Turkman tribes, probably descendants of the Mongols who had invaded and brutally subdued vast areas of Asia during the 12th and 13th centuries. The Turkmans maintained their own culture, though Muslims. The women, fine-limbed with pale skin and high cheekbones unlike Persians, wore layers of colourful skirts and long, fringed shawls printed or embroidered in brilliantly coloured floral patterns and falling to the knees. Their version of Islamic dress, which at least accommodated some colour and personal flair, appealed to me much more than the black chadour. The men bore themselves proudly in their high boots and baggy trousers made of coarsely woven wool, their stature exaggerated by tall, rounded hats of karakul fur from newborn Persian lambs.

Arash and his carload drove ahead of us, and stopped beyond each roadblock, ostensibly for chai from a thermos, but in fact to wait for us and ensure that we passed through without any problems.

At one of the blocks a young guard in his green uniform began to question Bijan. By now I could understand a few of his words.

'Zaneh kieh? (Who is this woman?)'

'Khanomam. (My wife.)'

'Documents a mari bede. Madarek edze vag dari? (Have you got your marriage certificate? Please show me.)'

I had covered myself thoroughly before we arrived at the checkpoint, pulling my scarf well forward to hide most of my face, for Bijan always seemed to know when the roadblocks were coming up although there was no written warning. I felt my body trembling but bowed my head and tried to look like a coy and modest Persian bride. I could see Arash's white car parked beside the road some distance ahead of us.

Suddenly Bijan broke into a loud and aggressive torrent of words, his hands wildly gesticulating as if he were outraged. I sat in stunned terror. Then, as abruptly, the guard mumbled a few words and, with head lowered, retreated to the edge of the road and beckoned us on. As we drove past

Arash and his friends, Bijan threw them a broad grin, quietly mouthing, 'Khoda re shokre. (Thank God.)' Once around the next corner and out of sight of the guard I raised my head and sought an explanation. Bijan was chuckling.

'Well, I realised that it could be very tricky as we don't have any marriage documents, so I told the guard that you had travelled all the way out from England to be my wife, and as Iranians didn't we wish to show foreigners the best side of our country and our ways? I appealed to the fact that he is first an Iranian, and only second a Revolutionary Guard, and that, as Iranians are renowned for their hospitality, he must surely wish to welcome you. I told him that I was outraged that, along with all the other problems you have to face in living in Iran, you also have to face rude and demanding officials who do not take your husband's word as that of a gentleman.'

As a result of this psychological tour de force the guard had apologised for asking to see the documents and even wished us a long and happy marriage and me a pleasant stay in Iran! How ludicrous that the formidable guard with his machinegun should have bowed down and apologised.

'But,' I said, 'it was very risky, there was another guard sitting in the cabin, watching the whole performance. It could easily have backfired.'

'Yes, you're right, but I had to take a chance. You see, these people often take the law into their own hands and dish out the punishment they see fit. They may never have waited to check with the mullah to see if in fact we were married.'

'So even our temporary marriage doesn't fully protect us?'

'I guess not, in fact. But listen, I know my countrymen and I trust myself and my friends enough to be sure that you would not come to any harm. Otherwise, I would never have asked you to come to this country.'

'But they've got the guns. What help could your friends have been if they had threatened us?'

Bijan replied after a long pause. 'There is a mentality behind most of these people, a basic motivation, and I feel I understand it well enough to deal with it.'

I was not at all sure. Hadn't his countrymen taken him by surprise lately? Could he have predicted the way things had turned out here recently? I knew he took risks, had done so as long as I had known him. But I had come because I trusted his judgment, because I trusted him. Perhaps I had been foolish to be so trusting.

Bijan gently brought the car to a halt at the side of the road and turned to look at me. His friends passed us waving and tooting, and sailed on around the next corner.

'For all that time when you were willing to come, I warned you against it. In fact, I wouldn't have helped you, because I didn't feel capable of taking care of you here. I would have been concerned for your safety. But now after living here for three years, while to an outsider it may seem that these people act without rhyme or reason, I know they are actually very predictable. I understand them now and I know how to handle them. But more, much more than that, I trust that we are protected. I feel perfectly safe. With our will and our faith, we will both be protected.'

For the first time I fully understood in my gut that there was danger here, that it was not just something people talked about, or a newsreel shot in a country of strife. I felt as if I should protest, as if I should demand more guarantees. Why then was I beginning to feel strangely safe? Life had already dealt me blows and I knew I was not exempt from further tragedy. Yet a kind of acceptance dawned that tragedy and disaster were not my due here.

Certainly Bijan was an optimist and sometimes his plans did not eventuate. Yet I had always, until this day, felt safe with him. He was one of the luckiest people I had ever met. I often had the feeling that he simply moved in a warm and comfortable stream of life, where what he needed came to him, and problems were resolved effortlessly. The last few years had not allowed him such freedom, and life had been a rocky road, but still I saw the same attitude of faith in himself, in his fellow man and in life itself. He did not accept any of the religious dogma that haunted his beloved country now. He was a rebel, but his rebellion was not to join the Mujaheddin and fight against the regime, but to live the way he wanted to, no matter what the circumstances.

His mother had told me how, as a boy, he had been the only one of the family who refused to go to the mosque, to fast and to observe the other

Islamic rituals. Yet Allah was a very important part of his thoughts and his life. He believed that laughter was more Allah's wish for us than penance, pain and martyrdom. So that, even within the strict confines of the Islamic state and the fervour of its leaders, he treated life as a game, and he played, at times dangerously. Being his woman, I was naturally caught up in those gambles. Yet I had an instinct that, in some incomprehensible way, I was protected by more than just Bijan and his friends.

CHAPTER 7

MY NEW HOME

After some hours we left behind the lush fields dotted with generous walnut trees and groves of old oaks, once the haunt of bears, deer, panthers and lynx, those animals so prominent in the famous hunting miniatures of Iran. The land through which we now travelled soon changed to the sort of moonscape on which I had looked down from the aircraft. As we passed over a wide plain between two ranges of mountains, Bijan pointed out the border with the Soviet Union, where, before the revolution, American surveillance bases had monitored enemy activity. Iran, formerly so strongly dedicated by the Shah to supporting United States foreign policy, would have been extremely vulnerable had the Cold War turned hot.

It was a lonely landscape, and as we passed a woman on foot, I wondered where she had come from and where she was going, for there were no villages for many miles and the barren land looked as if it could not support any life. But soon after, on a high and windy ridge, we saw boxes of grapes for sale and stopped to buy. A boy appeared as from nowhere. He had been hiding from the wind in an underground shelter. I had never seen such grapes: as long as fingers, pink and almost translucent. I had not realised that Iran with its hot summers and very cold winters was ideal for grapes. I had not connected the shiraz grape, so venerated by viticulturists, with the city in the south of Iran where it originated.

MY NEW HOME

Between bunches of luscious grapes, Bijan chewed sunflower seeds to help him keep awake. He tried to teach me how to separate out the husk from the edible seed with my tongue, but I never got the knack. At last I slept, stunned by the immensity, the emptiness, and woke in the early hours of the morning for the approach to Mashad. Five kilometres of huge poplars formed an arch over the grand double highway, white trunks gleaming in the headlights, leaves catching the light as they fell like twirling moths to be crunched under the tyres.

As we entered the walled city I tried to comprehend, with feelings of disbelief mingled with excitement, that this city of mosques and poplars, of pilgrims and saints, was to be my home.

Even at that hour Bijan took the long way home, through the old part of town, circling the ring road that enclosed Iran's holiest site, the tomb of Imam Reza, known as Haram. I glimpsed the gold-covered dome, all lit up, and the high minarets, fingers pointing towards God.

We pulled into a narrow alley and stopped before an arched metal gate in a high concrete wall.

Bijan pushed open the gate and, taking me by the hand, led me into a spacious courtyard. It was lit by a single outdoor lamp, and surrounded on three sides by walls and on the fourth by the house. The courtyard was paved except for a central area of garden dotted with trees and rose bushes, which radiated around a shallow pool, its water glistening under the gentle play of a fountain. As we circled the garden Bijan pointed out several fruit trees – cherry, apricot, blackcurrant – as well as a thriving herb patch. He plucked a late rose, heavy-petalled and full-scented. I breathed in its fragrance as we climbed the low steps onto the mosaic terrace.

Enchanted, I turned to look back over the garden, imagining how welcoming it would be in the heat of summer, with its shade and the music of running water, those gifts of nature most treasured by the people of desert lands.

Bijan had grown up in this house, an imposing residence built for a prosperous family by a noted architect in the early 1950s. The garden then had been much larger and on the outskirts of town. In fact Bijan remembered a young tiger once being found in it!

In those days the house, with its thick walls insulated to make it warm in winter and cold in summer in this country of extreme temperatures, its high ceilings, marble halls and numerous bathrooms, had been fully utilised. But now the upper floors, and part of the lower, had been rented out, leaving a small secluded apartment to be our home.

We entered the house through sliding glass doors leading into the main room. Richly carpeted in the deep red and blue rugs of Mashad, the room had white walls draped with gorgeous handmade cloths and kilims hung on brass rods. Turkman swabs lined the walls, a round walnut table with four handsome chairs stood in one corner and a woodstove in the other. The elaborate brass samovar had a stand of its own and was soon happily gurgling away. Delicate handblown glass lampshades tinged the light with pale hues of pink and blue.

The size of the kitchen, off to one side of this main room, provided a surprise. It was tiny. Perhaps it had originally been a sort of cupboard or storage area. Just over a metre wide and three metres long, its only windows were three narrow openings like arrow slits forming deep cavities in the massive outer wall. Handmade ceramics and gleaming old pots in brass and copper lined the shelves against the whitewashed walls. It was an attractive room, but I could imagine myself in quite a state trying to prepare a typical Persian feast! There was little bench space, and really only room for one person.

The bathroom was much larger than the kitchen, entirely tiled and with a central drain – a fine idea, I thought, imagining myself splashing around without the worry of flooding the floor. A traditional toilet with tap and hose, the Eastern equivalent of the bidet, occupied one corner. A primitive gas water heater, which needed to be lit each time hot water was required, took up another.

The only other room was the bedroom. This featured a low bed, a generous wardrobe, a tall chest of drawers and an oval mirror set in a finely wrought silver frame standing on a low inlaid table. Bijan told me how he had sought out antiques, most of them Russian, and restored them in his workshop at the end of the garden, remembering my taste for beautiful old furniture. His friends, inspired by his energy and enthusiasm, had worked with him at redecorating the apartment in time for my arrival.

As I wandered through the rooms I could see Bijan's personal touch everywhere. His love of the old and the unusual was evident, his eye for handcrafted excellence sure, and uncommon in Iranians, most of whom were bored with the traditional pieces and sought a modern showy look.

There was little left of the night, but I slept and slept far into the next day, my body fitted into the protective curve of Bijan's. I woke with no confusion, no fears. I knew where I was and it was where I wanted to be.

On rising, my first duty was to meet Bijan's father, who had stayed in Mashad while his wife had come to meet me in Tehran. His was a solitary life of reading and prayer and daily attendance at the mosque.

Bijan let us into his parents' home, which was next door, having been built in the grounds of the family home when they needed to move to a smaller place. It was quite bare except for the many carpets. No beds, chairs or tables – only built-in cupboards and shelves.

They were seated cross-legged on the floor, enjoying their evening sham: tea and a light snack. Babajan rose to greet me with a beaming smile – Bijan's smile, I thought. He kissed me on both cheeks, holding my hands, and greeted me in Farsi. Then he spoke to me in his few words of English, practised in advance probably.

'Anna, I love Essa.' As a good Muslim he would indeed venerate Essa (Jesus), a prophet of Islam, but I think this was his way of telling me that I, presumably a follower of Jesus from a Christian country, was being welcomed by him. He then pressed a little silver crucifix into my hand as a gift, with a very sweet smile. I was touched by his way of making me feel that I was accepted.

A huge man, with clear, unwrinkled olive skin and greying hair, he was still very handsome though in his late sixties. I understood now his nickname of 'the laughing man', for he had an air of lightness about him, and his smile did not fade as he invited me to sit near him.

I had learned from Bijan that his father was a Kurd, from that proud nation that had long fought for recognition of its identity by the regimes of Iraq and Turkey. Several centuries ago a number of Kurdish families had been persuaded by the great Shah Abbas to leave Kurdistan and settle, in return for land grants, in the north-east area of Iran. They were to be a buffer of warriors against the Turkmans, who for centuries had plagued the plainsmen by carrying off their livestock and women. This resettlement had been advantageous to Babajan's forebears, and his family still owned land in the north. However, he had made his career in Mashad, in administration of the Imam Reza Foundation, which governed Haram and dispensed its enormous wealth to charitable institutions. He had a highly developed aesthetic sense, and had been involved in the establishment of the Museum of Persian Crafts at Haram. He had his own fine collection of glass and porcelain lining the walls of his bedroom. Rosewater bottles, slender and curvaceous like voluptuous women, came from different areas of the Middle East, while the glassware was mainly of Russian origin. He treasured these finely crafted objects and handled them with great care.

His five children had been well provided for with a prime piece of land each, in Mashad. He had supported two of them in tertiary training abroad. Though he and his wife chose to live simply, they were by Western standards relatively wealthy.

I had come to Iran knowing only that Bijan's family were educated professional people, like my own, and believing that a similarity of backgrounds would be a help in overcoming the obstacles of a cross-cultural marriage. That there was also wealth was an added bonus.

Babajan was a contented man, committed to his religion, and mostly undisturbed by the changes the revolution had brought about. I never heard him or Mamajan pass judgment on either the Shah or Khomeyni. Perhaps they trusted the process of their country's evolution. But they were greatly troubled by the pointless war against Iraq, with its waste of human lives for political ends. And three of their grandsons were approaching the age of call-up. The revolution had been necessary; the war was not.

As we drank tea, Babajan introduced what was to become one of his favourite topics: Bijan's refusal to choose any girl but me. Bijan had told me that during the years we had been parted, his mother and sisters had paraded before him a constant stream of the most eligible young women in Mashad and Tehran, hoping one would catch his eye or his heart. They wanted him to forget about me, this foreigner who would no doubt persuade him to leave Iran again.

Because Bijan held a degree from abroad, he was labelled 'mohandes', which vaguely translated as graduate engineer. This made him a very desirable catch. As well, he came from a respected family, was good-natured and stunningly handsome. But he was also strong-minded, and did not succumb to the women's meddling in his decisions.

Insecure as I already felt, with so many eyes appraising me, I was always secretly distressed at Babajan's insistence on bringing this subject up again and again in the following months. I never doubted Bijan's love, but, isolated from my own family, I needed to feel his family's support. This was given initially to please Bijan, but it took a long and lonely time for them to accept me in total sincerity. Later I saw that they were surprised at our co-operation, and our closeness as companions. Bijan would help me with the cooking, I would help him fulfill urgent orders at the factory. I knew more about his finances than most Persian wives would ever be allowed or want to.

So when his sisters encouraged me to demand more from him, – jewellery, a new car, imported clothes – I ignored their advice. I was well aware of the difficulty of running a business in unstable conditions, and of the stressful world that awaited Bijan every time he set foot outside our gate. We were partners, our roles overlapping, as we built our lives together. I came to realise that such partnerships within a marriage were rare indeed in Iran.

CHAPTER 8

GHOSTS FROM THE PAST

Within a few days I had made the little apartment my home and introduced a womanly touch, with flowers in the vases and small ornaments and photos I had brought with me. Bijan spent several days at home before returning to his work as a paint manufacturer. He had started this business when work in his own field of computer technology was found to be unavailable.

As we lay on the grass, looking at the sky through the autumn-tinged leaves of the cherry trees, he revealed that he felt I had already brought great riches into his life.

We talked about our past lives and opened up to each other more than we ever had. Before he met me Bijan said he had dated many girls but never found one he could consider for a long-term relationship. I had only really loved one other man and I had never told him about James. Now I felt it was time to do so.

James and I knew each other before we left school. We had met at a ballroom dancing class. He was good-looking: tall and tanned from sailing and skiing. James was a year ahead of me and when I went south to Otago University he was in his second year at Auckland Medical School. We wrote letters and saw each other in the holidays, but because I missed him so much I decided to continue my university studies in Auckland. But the student lifestyle in Auckland was very different. I had lived in a student hostel in Dunedin and had a wonderful year, lots of parties and the sort of pranks students get up to. I don't know how I managed to get good marks because I didn't do much work.

At Auckland I was bored. There wasn't much going on except lectures, the lecturers seemed uninspired, and the subjects didn't seem to have much bearing on real life. It was the wrong time and place for me, after all those years at school when I had studied hard and been a model student. I left, gave up my bursary and got a job at a nightclub.

'You can imagine the scene I had to face at home!' I said. Bijan laughed; he had been through the same sort of thing with his parents.

But at the end of the year it wasn't funny because James failed his exams and I couldn't help feeling some responsibility. There we were, two 'failures'.

'I could never see you as a failure, Anna,' Bijan interrupted.

At that point James and I decided to travel, first to Australia, where we got work on my uncle's farm near Geelong. But before long we started having rows. James would go silent, and refuse to tell me what was the matter. I think the way he was brought up men weren't supposed to show emotions. They could get worked up about football or cricket, but not anything else. Somehow it always ended up with me feeling guilty if we had a row, though I never could figure out what it was I was doing that was wrong. Things got really bad.

We planned to hitch-hike to Darwin, but before we left Geelong a letter came from my mother. Dad was away in Norway at a conference and she was considering joining him in Geneva at Uncle John's. Her letter got me thinking, and when we were dropped off at a dusty little settlement in the Outback I rang her from a phone box. I told her I needed to break from James. I had enough money – just – to get to Geneva and I knew he did not. I asked her to meet me there. I put her on the spot, but she understood about James and I heard a 'yes' just before all my coins ran out.

In Darwin I bought a ticket for the first flight out to Europe. I was afraid that if I stopped to think about what I was doing I would change my mind. It was one of the hardest things I've ever had to do, leaving him in that airport at Darwin. I think I cried all the way to Rome, but as the train to Switzerland travelled through the absolutely unbelievable alpine scenery I stopped crying. And when I arrived in Geneva, there was Mum waiting at the railway station. From then on, I never looked back. From there we went to England, to Gail, Trilby – and Bijan.

Bijan's only comment at the end of my story was that maybe he ought to be jealous of James, but he could only thank him for being indirectly the cause of our meeting!

Now in Mashad we reminisced about our time in Derby. We had found a little flat and once more I had worked as a waitress while Bijan continued his studies at the polytech. He recalled how he would smell the bread baking as he rounded the corner coming home to our flat. I would always be there, in pinafore and pigtails, preparing something delicious for our evening meal. We explored the countryside of Derbyshire, revelling in the wilderness of the downs, and the steep valleys where fast-flowing streams had powered the first mills of the Industrial Revolution. With Trilby and Ahmed we must have made a striking quartet: the two handsome 'Persian princes', Trilby who looked like Elizabeth Taylor playing queen of the gypsies, and myself, tall, slim, with long hair bleached flaxen by the Australian sun, and looking out on the world from huge soulful 'Bette Davis' eyes. Galushka loved us: we were her 'fabulous four'.

The following year we holidayed in Spain and Morocco. But then came news from home to disturb our peace. My father wrote that he had decided to leave my mother, no reasons given. When I rang home my mother was so distraught she could hardly speak. She was in deep shock after what she had perceived as 27 years of a happy and co-operative marriage.

Bijan had nearly finished his course. He promised me he would follow me to New Zealand very soon. He did, and when he arrived on New Year's Day, 1979, at the family's beach cottage, he was wearing Baluchi pants, gathered at the waist and slim at the ankle, and a loose top, all in fine black muslin. No-one as interesting as this had been seen at the cottage since Queen Salote of Tonga, for whom a specially large hipbath had been made that still hung on a wall in memory of her visit many years before! Bijan was an instant hit with his exotic looks, impeccable manners and upper-class English accent. He made a particular impression on Paulo, my younger brother, then just 13 and probably on the lookout for a male role-model.

We had nearly a year together in Auckland – Bijan, me and Azizam, our beloved black cat. Nearly every Sunday we would go to Titirangi to my family home, now strangely empty without my father, and Bijan would take over the kitchen and produce a Persian feast. Afterwards he would take on Paulo at table tennis or pool. We both knew that these visits gave my mother and Paulo something to look forward to over a difficult time for them both.

But the day came when Bijan knew he must return to Iran, for he had had little news since the revolution. After he left I got a job teaching deportment and modelling skills but could not settle. Then one day I heard from a neighbour's daughter who worked on an Italian cruise liner that attractive young women were needed as stewardesses and waitresses for the round trip in the Pacific. I signed on and was shown my quarters, a cramped cabin for four girls in the bowels of the ship. To reach it we had to pass the morgue and the jail, where one inmate or another would always call out suggestive remarks as we passed the small open grille in the door.

It was a strange adventure. Life on board was often fun. A team of us practised the cancan and the tarantella to entertain the passengers. I enjoyed the brief interludes on shore in the tropics, and when we called back in Auckland for two nights, there were Mother and Paulo waiting on the wharf. Bijan smiled when I repeated later the conversation we had overheard between two tourists, probably father and son, on a German liner docked alongside. They didn't realise that Mum understood German, and when one said to the other, 'You have the young one, and I'll take the mother,' they were somewhat embarrassed at our laughter.

But all too soon it was time to sail again. My very last glimpse of Paulo as the ship gathered speed was of a tiny figure waving from the end of the wharf. I watched till I could no longer see the speck that was my darling brother. I didn't know that I was never to see him again.

The air-conditioning on board did not suit my health, for since childhood I had suffered from trouble with my lungs, and I got several attacks of bronchitis. The arrogant Italian doctor became even more indignantly uncooperative when I described to him the treatment that my father, a specialist in chest medicine, would have prescribed for me. I jumped ship in Sydney on the second voyage.

It was several days later that Bijan broached the subject of Paulo's death. It had been in the air, but neither perhaps felt secure enough in our newly found relationship to open it up. Bijan asked me how I had learned the news.

As I had told him earlier, I had left the ship in Sydney, got a menial job immediately and joined a household of young people. One evening when I arrived home I found them all waiting for me, as well as a young doctor who I found out later had been asked to come along in case I needed to be sedated. I was to ring home. I did, and learned that Paulo had died earlier in the day. My flatmates had already secured a booking on the next flight to New Zealand, and after a sleepless night I flew home. One of the things that stood out in my memory of that terrible flight was how considerate everyone was. I was given a single seat on the aircraft and shepherded swiftly through immigration and customs and out a side door, where Mother and my sister Lizzie were waiting, with Uncle Den in the car a few yards away. As we drove off Lizzie told me, her voice harsh with emotion, that Paulo had hanged himself. Held between my mother and my sister I fainted with shock – a momentary respite from the truth I had to face.

The next few days passed in a blur of faces, phone calls, and flower deliveries. Strangers, friends of Mother's I had never met, seemed to be running the household. Each night young cousins and friends found a place for their sleeping bags on the floor beside the fire. Dad arrived home from overseas but we couldn't hold the funeral until we found my brother Matt, who was somewhere in the South Island. Radio messages and advertisements in all the main newspapers brought no news. Two spiritual mediums were working on trying to locate him.

Eventually one reported that he was working with wood, and the other said one word had come to her: Manaroa. We discovered that this was a small settlement in Kenepuru Sound, in Marlborough. Mother rang a friend in Nelson, who confirmed with the police that there was a commune near Manaroa. A police launch visited and found that Matt was indeed living there, but that he was away in Blenheim dismantling an old house. He was at that very time driving a truck back along the many miles of dusty road bringing the wood to the commune. When he arrived and received the message it was already dark and there was not enough petrol left in the truck to make the trip to Picton. He set out to walk the 50-odd kilometres and by a miracle, on that isolated road, got a lift. He caught the last ferry, arrived in Wellington, waited till the post office opened, drew out some money and caught the next flight home. He arrived with what he stood up in, pale and silent.

When Paulo was brought home in a coffin for the funeral I couldn't look at him. That marble-white face, the hands I had loved folded on his chest. Mother sat with him and his friends came, each bringing some small offering to put in his coffin: a flower, a painting, a leaf, a bird's nest, a poem, a little pot from his friend in the pottery class. It was midwinter but the sun shone, the tuis left their hiding places and from the towering kauri trees added their chorus to the readings, which were mainly of his own poems. His favourite music, the slow movement from Beethoven's Fifth Piano Concerto, played as we carried him to the waiting hearse.

I cried and cried in Bijan's arms. I felt the tears burn my cheeks, the constriction in my throat and the long familiar ache in the region of my heart. And the pain was made even more acute by my feeling that perhaps I had deserted my little brother. Would things have been different if I had stayed behind and supported him and my mother through a hard time?

Bijan cried with me, helping me to understand that I could not take responsibility for others' actions. If I continued on this path, I would never be free of anguish. Gently, patiently, he helped me to begin to look forward again, to put the past behind me.

CHAPTER 9

MASHAD, THE HOLY CITY

There were many adventures Bijan wanted me to share: visits to local villages; camping trips to rivers and mountains; exploring a long-deserted 12th-century caravanserai on the historic Silk Road near the border of Turkmanestan; the great monument to the poet Ferdousi marking the site of Tus, his home town which over the centuries had been reduced to a mere mound in the landscape; Isfahan with its splendid architecture from the 17th century; Persepolis – Takteh Jamshied they called it, the Seat of Kings – near Shiraz, where we would also see the tombs of the poets Hafiz and Sa'di; Neyshabur, home of Omar Khayyam and the place where the finest turquoise was mined.

During those first days he also escorted me around Mashad, and explained the religious significance of this holy city. The Shiite Muslims, from the time of the schism between Sunni and Shia, honoured their Imam as Allah's vice-regent. So when the eighth Imam, Reza, was murdered for political reasons in 765 AD the site of the crime became sanctified. Gradually there grew up what was really a city within a city dominated by the tomb itself, lying under its gold cupola between the two golden minarets. Another mosque dedicated to the saint's sister, and considered to be the finest example of its kind in the world, shared the sacred area with libraries, schools and seminaries, museums, hostels and a refectory for pilgrims. There were three vast courtyards, with fountains and ablution pools, as well as all the offices required to manage the enormous wealth of the Imam Reza Foundation, which was said to rival that of the Vatican. Indeed, these two establishments were probably comparable in many other ways.

Muslims are required by their faith to make pilgrimages. As one of the principal sites for pilgrimage, Mashad, the city that developed around the tomb, grew in wealth and stature to become Iran's second city.

Being the centre of pilgrimage it was fanatically orthodox. Even in the days of the Shah, when religious observance was relaxed by all but the most sincere believers and Western standards prevailed in the big cities, foreigners ignoring Muslim rules of conduct and dress could expect a very aggressive reception here. I remembered a New Zealand traveller telling me how she had been stoned and hissed at when she descended from a bus in Mashad wearing shorts.

How strange to realise that my man, whom I thought I knew so well, had been brought up in this most alien of cities, a setting so utterly different from my own background. For me, how wonderful that in all this huge country, the place I was destined to live was within a kilometre of its holiest site.

Knowing that to ignore Islamic rules in such circumstances would have been destructive to myself and the family harbouring me, I felt myself an observer. I did not feel repressed or resentful that, as a woman from another culture, I too had to cover my hair and observe strict modes of behaviour. I was happy to be a passive participant in the great drama being enacted about me. I relished the chance to watch, to drink in all that was bewildering, disturbing, beautiful.

It was Mamajan who first took me into Haram, for, as men and women are separated inside the shrine complex, it was necessary for me to have a woman to guide me. She fitted me out with an extra head covering to wear under the chadour in case it slipped a little. She instructed me to keep silent, so that I would not be recognised as a foreigner from the West.

My first impression, on entering by way of one of the enormous courtyards, was of the many different races gathering there. I saw the ebony skin of Africans, the slit-eyed mongoloid features of the Central Asiatics, the baggy trousers and turbans of Afghanis, the differently draped veils and head coverings of Pakistani and Bahraini women, the hawk-like faces of Saudis in their snowy white robes.

So many faces bore the stamp of hardship and resignation, yet were lit up in the act of prayer and contemplation. Faces stripped of self-consciousness, openly revealing the emotional impact of the experience of pilgrimage.

The blind, crippled and war-wounded were gathered together near one of the walls of the inner complex, with a strip of cloth or string attached at one end to their body and at the other end to a grille in the wall. Lying, sitting, sleeping, some attended by family members, all waited for a miracle.

Two women were pouring water on the ground in one of the courtyards and I asked Mamajan what they were doing. She explained, in a mixture of mime and words, as was her way when I was learning the language, that there were many people buried in the catacombs beneath the courtyards. These women were purifying the place beneath which their loved one lay. After a pause she went on to tell me that she and Babajan had places waiting there for them.

Four times, while I was looking in another direction, Mamajan had to pull me out of the way of chanting men running swiftly through the courtyards taking a corpse in a long cloth-covered box for a final blessing at the tomb.

In yet another courtyard a circle of young men with red bands around their heads scourged their own backs with chains through holes in their black shirts, as their leader shouted encouragement and clashed cymbals. Mamajan explained that they were preparing for martyrdom in the war. The fierceness with which they flayed themselves, and the force of their voices, reminded me of the Maori haka.

There were many mullahs in their white turbans and brown capes. I saw one with a black turban, the sign that he was a descendant of Muhammad, according to Mamajan.

We came at last to the building in which the tomb was housed. Like everyone else, we removed our shoes and kissed the gold doors. Inside was a dazzling scene. The upper walls and high ceilings of this cavernous space were covered by millions of tiny mirrors, all set at different angles to catch the light from the huge chandeliers. The lower walls and arches, leading from hall to hall, were richly decorated with mosaics of twining arabesques and sayings from the Koran in Kufic script. There were soft carpets underfoot, incense in the air and the scent of rosewater, which Mamajan told me was used instead of water for cleaning inside Haram.

The tomb itself was inside a gold-grilled cage; this much I could see from behind the press of women trying to get near enough to touch it or, if possible, kiss it. There were babies being passed forward from hand to hand over the heads of the crowd. Then one quite large child, a cripple, was lifted up and began her precarious journey towards the cage. All I could see were hands stretched out towards the tomb, or gripping the bars. All I could hear was the moaning, wailing and sobbing of women, the cries of the children, and from the other side of the cage, barricaded off from where we were, the voices of the men pressing towards the tomb from the opposite direction. All I could feel was the press of sweating bodies against my own as we were pushed forward by the heaving mass from behind. I felt totally at the mercy of the will of the crowd and moved forward with it, elbowed and squeezed on all sides. Mamajan, sensing the beginnings of panic in me, dragged me from the crush before I reached the cage. For this I was grateful, because the intensity of emotion on all sides was not easy to bear.

She took me into one of the halls reserved for women, where they can change from travelling clothes into white garments for the visit to the tomb, feed their babies, or simply rest, as we did. I lay down on the floor, my head in Mamajan's lap, and slept, exhausted, for a little time.

Outside again, we collected our shoes and our wits and sat for a while near one of the fountains that are used for ablutions before prayer. Men were washing their arms and faces, and rubbing wet hands through their hair. We watched a mullah arrive on a motorbike with a badly crippled woman on the back seat. Mamajan helped her get down because, she explained, the mullah was not allowed to touch the woman, even if she needed help. We left her, crawling forward on her hands and knees. I wondered how she would fare as she approached the tomb.

Babajan had arranged for me to be invited to lunch in the refectory, as an honour extended to a pilgrim from a Christian land. We joined the queue with our entrance tickets, watched by a crowd of people who obviously would like to have been in our place.

The refectory, designed to feed 1000 people at a sitting, is pleasantly appointed and spotlessly clean. The simple food of rice, a meat khoresh (stew), bread and abdug (diluted yoghurt as a drink) was more than we could eat so I slipped the remains of a slab of bread under my chadour, thinking of the hungry faces outside. When we came out I pulled the bread in half and handed it to two of the waiting women. Others tried to grab it from them and a fight erupted around us. The bread was evidently precious, not as something to eat but as something from Haram. Mamajan was very cross with me, and told me off with wagging finger and stern eyes. I realised that taking such an initiative, when I did not know the implications, was a stupid thing to do. I learned my lesson but secretly had to smile, remembering the spectacle of those women chasing each other around like a flock of hungry seagulls.

I went back to Haram many times, sometimes by myself, at different times of the day, in different seasons. Every time was different. Every time I saw a new aspect of Islam. Every time I was impressed by the fervour of the pilgrims, something the Christian world had all but left behind. For good or for ill? That I could never decide.

Mashad itself was built on a high plateau between the Alborz Range in the west and in the east the Hindu Kush, which rose over the border in Afghanistan about 100 kilometres away. It had been founded at least a thousand years ago, clustered around the tomb and the old bazaar.

I particularly loved some of the older homes where the ornamental use of bricks was the main decorative feature, but most of the affluent modern exteriors were clad in marble or mosaic. Few of the very old wooden houses remained. Each home opened into a private courtyard, usually paved, with a decorative pond and perhaps a fountain to provide the sound of running water. The beauty of the homes was tucked away behind high walls, and many of the streets were desolate and unattractive. However, tree planting on all the city's main highways and many of its lesser thoroughfares gave it dignity.

The chosen tree was mostly the immensely tall white poplar. This tree was not universally admired, however, as I learned from Bijan's brother one morning when he came to borrow our car. His own had been smashed during the night by a falling branch, and this kind of damage was common as the trees became brittle with age. Deep channels parallel to the footpaths watered the poplars' roots, cooling the atmosphere. The great arcades in spring were a mass of brilliant green as the new leaves come through, and in autumn filled the air with hushed tones and an abundance of falling leaves. Iran's second city was truly a city of trees.

It was a city I knew I would come to love – its buildings, its wide avenues, its vistas of distant mountains, and above all, the jewel of Haram at its heart.

CHAPTER 10

LEARNING TO FIT IN

On the long days after Bijan returned to work I enjoyed exploring those parts of Mashad I could reach on foot. Although there was a car for me, driving was a nerve-wracking experience. Everyone drove fast and traffic was not well controlled by lanes and traffic lights. And some male drivers definitely reacted aggressively to a woman driver. Besides this, the only maps available had all the street names written in the local alphabet, as were the street signs. But on foot I could not easily get lost.

Near our home a busy roundabout was ringed with little shops that met most of our needs: a butcher, two bakeries producing different types of bread, several greengrocers with their banks of herbs and piles of seasonal fruit and vegetables taking up large areas of the footpath, shops stocking barrels of grains and spices, a little cupboard shop stuffed full with haberdashery, and one I found hard to pass by. This was the confectioner's, displaying magnificent arrays of cakes, biscuits, pastries, shortbread in many shapes, and sweets. I was often hungry, with the new diet, and longed for something sweet, or something familiar. Images of Vegemite sandwiches, grilled bacon or a cold beer often filled my reveries.

Mamajan introduced me to the various shopkeepers who were her friends and could be trusted not to take advantage of my ignorance. I soon chose to go on my own, however, testing out my independence and my growing use of Farsi. Well covered in my sweeping chadour and armed with a hemp basket and a selection of Iranian money, tomans and rials, I would go shopping, pointing out the bread or herbs that I desired, then holding out a handful of coins and notes, which shrewd Mamajan would often check when I arrived home, until I understood the value of the different coins.

One of the shops was owned by a Mahmoud Agha,[9] a little old man who was so short I felt I was looking down on him from a great height. His shop was dark and tiny, like himself, and filled with the oddest assortment of goods: bleach and children's books, chewing gum and dried herbs fought for space on his shelves, while on the topmost one stood dusty bottles of rosewater. I wanted some rosewater but could not imagine how Mahmoud Agha would reach it as there was no ladder in sight. So I bought it elsewhere.

I often stopped at one or other of the two bakeries to watch the bread being made. The workers seemed gratified by my interest and welcomed me in, often testing their few words of English on me. In one of the bakeries the oven was a bricked cavern in the ground with a fire in the base. The bread stuck to, and was baked on, the sides of this great hole. The other had a glowing and roaring firebox into which the loaves were pushed on a shovel with a very long handle. The bread from both was delicious while still warm, but soon went stale. Bijan would pick up fresh bread on his way home in the evening.

My shopping expeditions were always saddened by the martyrs' photographs plastered on the walls. Often, too often, a new face would appear, and I would learn that he was the son or nephew of one of the shopkeepers, or someone who lived in the neighbourhood.

I had to walk a little distance to the next shopping centre to buy milk or yoghurt, which was ladled into a plastic bag to be carried home. Halfway along this street was a shrine on the footpath. It was a glass box on legs in a turquoise frame and contained a large framed photograph of a very young face, lit up by coloured electric bulbs. Fresh greenery was twined around it, and sometimes flowers. It stood there for 40 days. One night as we drove past I saw two young men asleep on the pavement beside the shrine. Perhaps they were young brothers, perhaps others preparing for martyrdom. How my heart ached for these young ones, remembering Paulo. I knew that within the walls of the home shut off from the street there must be great despair, especially for the women, for war has surely never meant glory to mothers.

The mosque always seemed to be part of every shopping centre. I learned from Daniel that in Islamic countries bazaar and mosque lived side by side, religion and commerce two sides of the same coin. In the past there would have been a caravanserai for travelling merchants to complete the trio.

The mosque at our roundabout was a plain concrete building with a loudspeaker over the entrance, for the taped call to prayer that reached every home. At this time the mosques also served as bases for the Revolutionary Guards, young men often without uniform and therefore indistinguishable from local boys, except that they carried guns. They invariably looked scruffy and unkempt, with unshaven faces and open-necked shirts, but I discovered that this appearance was intentional – they despised personal vanity. Also, shaving was considered one of the minor sins, which was why most clerics and government officials in Iran wore beards.

Often a canvas canopy would be set up outside the mosque, and demands made through the loudspeaker for shoppers to give generously towards the war effort. Offerings of money, gold, jewellery, ration tickets, food, blankets, anything of value was accepted. The government, its income from oil production drastically cut, could not have fought the war without this support.

Once a week Mamajan picked me up in her car to collect our rations from the government distribution centre. A blast of the horn outside my gate told me she was ready to go. The trip was always eventful. She would inevitably stall the car or collide with someone in a minor way, but no-one took it too seriously; every car on the road carried scars.

After much queuing, and hustling and cajoling the issuing officer (much to my embarrassment), she would always end up with slightly more than our share of the things that were rationed: butter, oil, soap, tobacco, tea, sugar and chickens. These goods were also available in the regular shops but at very much higher prices. Rationing was to protect the poor: the new regime needed the support of the poor. On the black market anything was available, from Scotch whisky to fancy cigarettes, so I was told, but at astronomical prices.

I always knew when it was Mamajan banging on my gate, for the sound

Street scene in Mashad. In the background is the gold dome of the shrine of Imam Reza, around which is built a huge religious complex.

Imam Khomeyni looked down from all public buildings.

An anti-American poster.

Martyr's shrine on the footpath.

Poster extolling the virtues of martyrdom.

ABOVE: Schoolgirls, two in chadour, one wearing the alternative, a loose coat and head scarf.

LEFT: An Afghani 'visitor', a refugee selling prayer beads.

In Golsara. Fatima practising her carpet-making skills.

A woman cooking the daily bread.

A housewife selecting her sabsi (green herbs).

Wife of the headman at Taher Abad washing clothes in the spring.

had a peremptory ring of authority. There she would be, with her chadour pulled tightly around her head and held between her teeth, while with her hands she would gesture her communication. 'Come for lunch.' 'I'll take you shopping.' 'Here is some food for you.' 'Let me come in.'

Often I felt she treated me like a six-year-old and I resented being bossed about. Her way was the only way, she always knew best – about everything. No argument or alternative could be considered. She was so strong that it was difficult, almost impossible, to prevail against her wishes or opinions. But I came to realise that this was the way she treated her daughters, and that her concern was out of a growing affection for me. I found that in our family (as in others I came to know well) tremendous respect was shown for the mother, the matriarchal figure, and her word was accepted as law in all matters relating to the home and the upbringing of the children, in which the man took no part.

In time I learned simply to give in, turn my face away and swallow my annoyance. But it was not easy.

We were regular visitors to each other's homes. She often sent Soraya to check that I was not feeling lonely on the long days while Bijan was working, for he would leave home before seven and return after dark. Occasionally he would come home for lunch and the siesta so loved by the Iranians.

Almost more than the days of exploring the outside world, I relished the days I had to myself, days that stretched out before me offering freedom – the freedom of solitude and silence, the freedom from schedules and time tables, the freedom from responsibility. Time. Time to watch the days move past, from cool morning to warm noon and on into nightfall; to watch the moods in my little garden, the flowers budding and opening, the leaves turning and falling. Time to watch the sparrows fly in and busily peck at the crumbs I put out for them, their feathered heads bobbing as they chattered and looked about them. Time to watch the wild cats, battle-scarred and proud, like the Afghan refugees I saw on Mashad's streets. The cats prowled along the courtyard wall, haughtily claiming their territory – cats that somehow survived the harsh winter months, as beggars and thieves, fearless and brazen in their contempt for everything but their own survival.

I often lay on the floor and listened to the pigeon, my invisible friend, which lived in the bricked-up chimney in my kitchen. For hour upon hour I would hear her cooing, utterly abandoned and ecstatic in the pleasure of her own music. How I longed for such abandonment, for the ability to give in my life as passionately and completely as the bird did in her song, teaching me to let go of cares and enjoy the moment.

An old woman, Soghra Khanum,[10] who had been a casual servant to the family for years, came now to help me in my home. It seemed the ultimate luxury and decadence, but I was glad to be relieved of the constant burden of housework. Dust blew in day after day from the dry plains, and autumn leaves littered the yard. There was always some chore to be attended to. So the woman came, speaking not a word of English and colouring her Farsi with a heavy accent. She was short and solid in her old shapeless clothes. From beneath her ruhsari, wisps of greying hair strayed over her weather-beaten forehead. She complained endlessly: about her poverty, about her miscarriages (which must have been long past!) and about how tough life was these days.

'Can I take one little carrot and a small potato for my boy? I haven't enough to feed him properly,' she whined each time before she left, and each time I disobeyed Mamajan's orders not to give her anything. I knew that her pathetic story was not as bad as she told it, for she wore gold and was well cared for by our family. Yet I was willing to play her game.

Together we swept the yard of leaves and dust, she holding the hose and me using the broom, and both getting wet in the process. But closeness comes from working together, even in such a simple task, and as we swept and washed she would recite prayers in a portentous voice and I would diligently imitate her. Our yard was filled with sounds of praise to God. Though I understood not one word, it felt good and it united me with this woman from another world.

We often breakfasted together, Soghra and I, for Bijan rose early and took breakfast with his parents next door, while I was still luxuriating in bed. We would sit together on the tiled terrace and share black tea, thin bread with clotted cream and home-made carrot or quince jam.

Soghra's scarf never left her head, and needed constant adjusting to stop it from slipping. She was a good Muslim in this regard – she was not tempting men to sin with the beauty of her grey locks! Yet when she washed our clothes in the big metal pan, squatting in the yard, her hands in the cold water from the garden tap, she would often strip off her dress and add it to the other articles, her plump sagging breasts nestled in her lap, bare for all to see. Once Bijan arrived when she was in this state of undress and her hand flew automatically to adjust her scarf while her breasts remained uncovered. I watched in amazement, also aware that an upper storey of the house was occupied by two young men who had a good view of the yard from their back windows.

Islam in Iran dictated that those parts of the body that most excited the male must not be revealed, yet surely the very act of hiding increased the desire to peep at the forbidden? It seemed to me that the Muslims may have created a vicious cycle. As a result of women being so well covered and so totally out of reach, perhaps men had become preoccupied with sex. In that case the severe restrictions on relationship between the sexes may indeed be necessary, for the protection of women.

Bijan had provided me with a copy of the Koran in Arabic and English, It had a concordance in the back that enabled me to look up any subject that puzzled me about Islam. However, I have to admit that there often seemed contradictions. Stories from the *Hadith*, writings about Muhammad's own life, provided a better insight into what Islam was all about. Muhammad had numerous wives, sometimes widows of his generals, sometimes women he married in order to forge an alliance. I gather that they formed a turbulent household and for whatever reason, Muhammad insisted that they be secluded from access to other men. But his divine instruction to other women was simply that they should be modest in dress and action. Only subsequently was this interpreted, by men, to mean that women's hair and bodies should be covered up, and that they should be segregated from men.

Soghra Khanum taught me many things about Islam. For instance, that clothes should be washed in running water. She also showed me how to wash the dishes more thoroughly – soaping first, then rinsing under the tap. I was quite shocked to learn that Iranians, and Muslims in general, considered Europeans slapdash, almost grubby. They themselves were obsessed with cleanliness, especially personal hygiene. Toilet paper was not generally used. Instead, a hose next to the toilet served to fill a jug with a long spout, for washing after using the toilet.

You always took your shoes off in an anteroom before entering the house (unless it was for a special party, when shoes were allowed). Well-organised households had racks for discarded shoes, and some even had a selection of slippers to choose from. Special plastic slip-ons were to be used in the kitchen, bathroom and toilet. Sometimes it seemed to me that I was forever taking off and putting on shoes.

However, I readily accepted all these new conventions, for I had to admit they were based on sound reasoning.

CHAPTER 11

OUT AND ABOUT

And so the days drew into weeks and the weeks drew into months. They said it was a particularly warm autumn. The weather was crisp and clear. I took long walks, exploring the streets near our home, delighting in the new sounds and sights: the Afghani refugees in their baggy trousers and loosely tied turbans; street vendors pushing carts piled high with produce as they called housewives out to buy, each with his own individual cry; nomad women dressed in bright colours and dripping in ancient silver, their hands stained with henna; wizened little men in ill-fitting suits riding enormous bicycles that looked as if they had come from a circus; and others on motorbikes carrying amazing loads such as ladders, and once even a sheep, on the petrol tank in front.

From the house I would hear the mournful cry '*Namaki!*'. I would hurry then to gather up all the left-over ends of bread and hasten down the lane in time to catch the 'salt man' in his cart pulled by a donkey. He would weigh the bread and give me a portion of rock salt in return.

As a newcomer I was not permitted to visit anyone, be they family or friends, until they had first called on me. I remember the first such visit very well, and it set the pattern for many more.

Hastily pulling on my headscarf as I went to respond to a tap on the gate, I opened it to find an attractive but quite unfamiliar face smiling at me over a bouquet. The stranger introduced herself as the wife of a doctor who had known Bijan from school days.

She removed her shoes, coat and ruhsari at the door, revealing gold bracelets, chains and earrings, and a smart frock. Her make-up was immaculate. In contrast, I was wearing jeans and neither make-up nor jewellery.

Relieved at the opportunity to do something, I made chai and filled a plate with delicate sweet biscuits flavoured with nuts and rosewater, fortunately bought that very morning at the confectioner's. Then, smiling at each other as we sipped our tea, we carried out a rather stilted conversation, as I drew her out about her family, her child, her life. With my limited grasp of Farsi we soon came to the end of the subjects we could discuss, and I was left smiling but tongue-tied, looking forward to the time when my guest would leave.

She was very inquisitive, but not about my life. What interested her, I began to realise, was what clothes I had brought with me. She examined the labels and, as they were foreign clothes, she offered me very high prices for them, even though they were far too small for her. She touched my hair and enquired if it was coloured, and eyed my belts with disbelief. She picked up my perfumes, and asked me if I had brought any fashion magazines. Of course I had not. Bijan had warned me that pictures of women with bare arms and legs would be confiscated by customs.

Finally the woman took her leave, after pinning me down to a date when she would collect me and take me to her home to show me her wedding album and meet her child.

After she left I felt I had been examined and found wanting. There had been no acceptance on her part, tacit or otherwise, that perhaps my priorities were different from hers.

As this was the first of many such visits, I soon learned to have the samovar boiling and keep a large crock of special biscuits on hand. Instead of getting around the house in my husband's oversized pyjamas I now dressed early in the day in an outfit suitable for socialising. I realised I was being looked over. Everyone was wondering what was so special about the foreign wife of the so eligible young mohandes.

Once the novelty had worn off I had fewer callers, which was a great relief. But one I always looked forward to seeing was Bijan's cousin, Goli, which means flower. Goli had been a medical student at the time of the revolution. Born into a prominent medical family, her one desire was to train in medicine in order to serve society. Her parents were extremely wealthy but Goli was acutely aware of social inequality, and had great sympathy for the poor. She wanted to know all about the state system of welfare for which New Zealand was famous, because it had been the first country in the world to introduce a free health and social security service.

As a student she had seen that all was not well in Iranian society and had become interested in the theories of socialism as a possible answer. Both socialist and communist factions were working to depose the Shah. But when Ayatollah Khomeyni came to power, all who had had dealings with either movement were suspect. Goli was expelled from the university and imprisoned for six months. During this time she underwent 'retraining', though she assured me she was never badly treated. When I met her, four years after the revolution, she was still hoping to be accepted back into her course, and was frustrated at being unable to get on with her life.

Her story made me realise how I had taken for granted and thus undervalued my right to education.

With Goli I was able to explore the vast Imam Reza bazaar[11] where, because of its proximity to Haram, and the religious orthodoxy of the bazaaris, we always wore chadour. But even when we were not going to the bazaar Goli always wore drab clothes in dark colours and was very quiet on the street, walking with downcast eyes and a serious expression. I remember her reply when I asked her why she would never wear a coloured ruhsari, for example.

'Anna, now that I have been released, everyone – the neighbours, the servants, the pasdaran who know me – everyone is watching to see if I have learned my lesson. If I'm given another chance to get back into university, what I say won't count; what these others say about me is what will count. I need to be seen as a model Muslim woman. I don't wear make-up because that's a giveaway. It means I haven't washed my face, therefore I can't have prayed. And I don't wear clothes that will attract men to look at me, or perfume – only rosewater is acceptable. According to Islam I'm guilty if, by my actions, I cause men even to think about having sex outside of marriage.'

Her explanation showed me once more the enormous cultural gulf between Islam and our Western ways. I felt this guilt was a terrible responsibility to place on women, and yet I saw how often women in my culture carelessly tantalised men through the way they behaved and dressed. It seemed to me that each culture might have something to learn from the other, but was covering up sex the answer? I felt it simply gave sex more importance, charging every contact between male and female with a degree of energy that was not always relevant to the situation.

The bazaar was housed in a very long, wide corridor composed of a series of high domes with skylights, and consisted of hundreds of little shops. These were selling oils and flower essences, natural plant medicines, carpets, fabrics, dried herbs and spices, bright Turkman shawls, prayer beads of plastic or semi-precious stones, costume jewellery as well as antique silver and gold, and all manner of goods unfamiliar to me. Quality and rubbish side by side. Because Imam Reza's tomb ranked second only to Mecca as a place of pilgrimage for Shiite Muslims, there was also every kind of tourist gimcrack. Pilgrims were said to number 15 million a year, more than the number who visited the Vatican or the Eiffel Tower.

With Goli's help I learned to bargain, and enjoy the game. I was forever being stopped by strangers who wanted to know where I came from. Their response to my answer, Zelande-No, was invariably enthusiastic, even though I doubt if many would have been able to pinpoint New Zealand on the map.

One day, when we were fossicking at the back of a fabric store in a side street, we unearthed a treasure trove, a huge carton of rolls of cloth, all jumbled together: chiffons, organzas, satins, silks, taffetas, lace, magnificently embroidered, sequinned, bejewelled, appliquéed, all obviously put away as inappropriate during the austere times of the revolution and forgotten. We asked the shopkeeper to bring them to the counter and within minutes were surrounded by a growing crowd of frenzied women fingering our finds, oohing and aahing, pulling them to the light to see the colours more truly, holding them up against their bodies.

Goli was not interested for herself, but I came away with a great booty, involving months of dressmaking to come, and leaving a delighted shopkeeper behind. It seemed that because I was a foreigner, anything that had my approval had to be 'right', so hungry were Iranian women for fashion news from the West.

It was indeed hard even for me to keep up with what was going on in the world outside Iran, in spite of letters from home. I never found any publications in English. I felt very isolated living in a country where I was unable to read the papers or even the street signs. We had a small portable radio on which, most nights, I caught the world news from the BBC. The cultured English voice, quavering across the immense distance and vying with the gabble of many foreign tongues, seemed to come from a different world.

Some afternoons I would go next door to Mamajan's house to watch the television news in English, often presented by a woman looking most demure with her securely tied ruhsari and downcast eyes. It was in three quarter-hour sections, the first section giving news from inside Iran, the second covering world events, while the third monitored the progress of the movement for Islamic fundamentalism in neighbouring countries by the Hezbollah (Party of God) and other missionary groups. It was made to sound like a worthy cause.

One of the first family gatherings I attended was the mourning ceremony on the seventh day after the death of Babajan's brother. He had had several wives and many children, so the drawing-room of the home where we gathered was full of women of various ages. All wore black, the older women in exquisite lacy chadours, while the younger ones, whose job was to serve the food, had mostly discarded theirs temporarily. After the meal we boarded a hired bus, men in front, women in the back seats. The bus driver and the men mumbled a prayer for a safe journey and we set off for the cemetery.

Here the veiled women crouched around the new grave, repeating prayers, while the men stood at a little distance, telling their prayer beads. As I had not known the dead man I felt out of place, and wandered into the part of the cemetery reserved for martyrs. As I walked between the rows of little glass shrines I noticed that sweets, dates and fresh fruit had been laid on some, and I was offered food by some mourners. Several families were there, celebrating the fortieth day after the martyrdom of their loved one. I well understood how these regular remembrance ceremonies could be a great help to the bereaved, who might otherwise feel flat and lonely after the high point of the funeral.

We often visited Nadia and Daniel in their lovely house, built just prior to the revolution. This was purposely left unfinished on the exterior in order to avoid angry attacks from people who were jealous of their affluence. For the same reason owners of expensive cars seldom took them out, choosing to drive instead the locally manufactured Paykan. Anyone with a lot of money was slightly suspect. Perhaps they had profited from some association with the Shah's family, which had controlled and benefited from most of the major financial transactions in the country and were consequently known as the 'thousands family'.

Sometimes we were invited to watch a video at Nadia's house, Daniel having gone to some trouble to find one in English for me. The first turned out to be *The Incredible Hulk*, while the second time we had to sit through six episodes of *Lassie*, trying to look enthralled for the sake of our hosts' feelings. We were really looking forward to watching *Gandhi*, but the video cassette was so worn that we had to give up after half an hour. It was the same with old pre-revolution tapes. Years of heavy use and retaping had distorted them almost beyond recognition.

Movie theatres provided a diet of films of war and propaganda – for mostly male audiences presumably, as I never saw a woman among the crowds waiting outside the cinemas. The men also had their football matches: at times I would hear the roar of male voices from some nearby stadium.

Bijan's aunt, Khalejan Mehri, was a very devout Muslim. She would sometimes hold meetings for her women friends and relatives, to which a mullah would be invited to speak about the faith, read from holy books, and exhort his hearers to give donations to the war effort. I arrived at my first such meeting wearing my coat and ruhsari, but these clothes were evidently not suitable to be worn in the presence of a mullah. So Mehri, who was an exceptionally tall woman, lent me one of her chadours and I spent much of the evening tripping over the voluminous folds while trying to look poised and comfortable.

I was invited back to the celebration of the battle of Kerbala. This time I was suitably dressed, and just as well, as it was a very grave occasion. The women all sat on the floor, weeping and crying out, as the mullah, seated on a black-draped chair, recounted in a voice that dropped to a whisper only to rise in a scream the story of the massacre of Hossein, Muhammad's rightful successor, and his followers. In the atmosphere of overwhelming grief I felt my own tears rising. This experience enabled me to understand a little how the pattern of grieving can be encouraged and carried on, generation after generation, for an event that, tragic as it was, happened, after all, 13 centuries ago. How sad that these techniques are used to keep ancient enmities alive.

After I met Vakhri, a beautician who had lived in England and the US, I realised how much I had missed friends I could really talk to without fearing I was saying the wrong thing. Vakhri was different. She had actually divorced her husband, not the other way around, and was therefore looked on socially as rather a 'loose' woman. I think Bijan's family probably disapproved of our friendship. However, I had a good excuse. Once a week I would go for a facial, and she would always leave a big space in her appointment book so that we could have time for a cup of coffee, a few laughs, and perhaps another episode of her soap-opera life story, which she related with great verve.

One of her stories revealed the kind of arrogant patronage that Iranians often told me they experienced when they travelled to the West. Vakhri was driving in London and had a minor accident involving another car. No great damage was done on either side but the other driver was furious and shouted at her that she had no right to drive in England, she should be riding a camel in the desert! 'They know nothing about Iran,' she said. 'They confuse us with Arabs, and they think we're all a bunch of savages in this part of the world.'

Vakhri totally approved of the 'new style' chadour I had made myself, inspired by European fashions of the past. It was black and covered the body totally, but to avoid having to hold it close under my chin I had attached a loose hood, which certainly covered the hair but framed the face more attractively. Whenever I wore it I would notice people, especially women, stopping in their tracks to stare. I didn't like this attention, so restricted myself to wearing it when we went to a restaurant for dinner or when I was visiting Vakhri.

Several times we met at a quite grand hotel, which we still referred to as the Hyatt, although it had been given a new revolutionary name. We sat outside in the garden restaurant and tried to imagine we were in Paris or San Francisco. Once I decided to be a bit naughty and wear sheer stockings to our rendezvous, but I was stopped at the door and refused entry.

Although Vakhri was great fun to be with mostly, she always became very tearful and silent at the mention of children and families. Her daughter was being brought up by her husband's family, as under Islamic law the child belongs to the father following a divorce, and she was seldom able to see her, let alone make any decisions about her future.

Usually, entertainment came down to dinners in private homes. My first attempt at hosting a dinner party was a most memorable failure. Our guests were Musa and Mitra from Tehran, and a local couple. In spite of the fact that Musa had helped Bijan obtain my visa into Iran, I didn't feel comfortable with him. I had never joined a women's movement, or particularly felt the need to be liberated, but I had always demanded respect as an equal from my male friends. Of equality between the sexes Musa knew little! It seemed that his wife existed to serve his needs. She did so splendidly but got little recognition. I felt very sorry for her. And I knew he did not approve of me, for he had arrived to greet me the first day in Tehran dressed in his best suit and cravat, bearing flowers, to find me pale, inappropriately dressed and suffering from culture shock. He had joked in a private aside to Bijan that he felt all the bother of importing me had hardly been worth it!

I was determined to impress him favourably this time, and so was thoroughly prepared when the guests arrived. The dinner, of roast lamb (not New Zealand lamb, which the butcher advised against as it was frozen), baked potatoes, steamed greens and carrots in orange sauce, was well under control. I acted the gracious hostess, handing around chai and individual plates of fruit and bowls of nuts.

However, when the meat came to be carved, it was found to be hardly cooked. The roast vegetables were tough, almost inedible. The guests had never been confronted before by bowls of carrots and leathery green beans and did not know what to do with them. However, there was no alternative but to eat what we could of the meal. Then my crowning omission came to light – I had forgotten to provide fresh bread, and the unleavened loaf I had bought that morning was already stale! It was an agonising evening for me, utterly bewildered and very close to tears as I was.

Later I learned that local meat needed many hours of cooking because the animals had to work so hard to forage, and that the vegetables, grown with little water, are only ever used in stews or soups. Classical Iranian cuisine took these limitations into consideration, but no-one had explained this to me. I believe that the great height above sea level also affected the way certain ingredients behaved. For instance, having managed to borrow that rare utensil, an egg-beater, from our neighbour in order to dazzle guests with a New Zealand speciality, pavlova, I found that the egg whites simply would not beat up into the stiff froth that I required.

I had always been known as a good cook, and had enjoyed preparing and cooking food since childhood. In Iran a woman is judged largely by her ability to cook well. I never quite recovered from this blow to my confidence and to my reputation.

In the end, having learned by trial and error that Iranians were not adventurous in their eating habits as they considered their cuisine the best in the world, I gave up all thought of introducing novelties, and learned to cook their way.

Fortunately for me our apartment was not large enough to accommodate the whole extended family for the weekly family luncheon. This was always held at one home or another on Jami (Friday), the weekly day of prayer and rest. Babajan and Daniel would have spent the morning at the Friday mosque. They would arrive and change into their comfortable 'house pyjamas', which Iranian men loved to wear indoors.

There was always one main dish with a rice base, such as estanboli polo (rice with beef and tomato), bagali polo (with broad beans and dill), or albaloo polo (with sour cherries). It would be served with a khoresh (stew) made with meat and vegetables or sometimes with fruit, such as khoreshe beh, using quinces. But my favourite was always fesenjan, a chicken stew made with pomegranate sauce and walnuts. These would be accompanied invariably by a large platter of sabsi,[12] which we ate by the handful, unleavened bread and abdug, a delicious drink made from diluted yoghurt, though even among the adults Coca-Cola was usually more popular. After a huge repast served on the sofreh, the generations would sort out. The adults prayed and napped while the children inevitably sprawled in front of television.

It was on these afternoons that I got to know Mehdi, Bijan's brother. On our way to Spain years earlier I had met him briefly in France, where he had been studying neurosurgery in Lyon.

Mehdi was an idealist, a humanitarian who cared little for money and worldly success. He was not outwardly religious, as were some other members of the family, but an ardent Muslim nevertheless. His interest in Islam was more from a social point of view than a religious one; he simply believed that Islam was a superior teaching, that the way of life it advocated was based on the highest ethical standards.

Before the revolution he had led student protests against the Shah, writing pamphlets, plays and poems. Bijan remembered the day two men in plain clothes came to the home and escorted Mehdi away. As he went he held a finger to his lips, gently demanding silence, and it was only then that Bijan understood what was happening. He ran to tell his mother but the car had already driven away.

His mother burned all the writings that may have incriminated Mehdi, and went every day to the Savak headquarters to get news of him. She was given no indication of what was happening to him but she never gave up. One day, several months later, Mehdi simply walked back into the house, thinner, paler, quieter than before.

Mehdi refused to tell the family what had happened to him in prison. They feared he may have been tortured but if this was true, he never spoke of it. But he agreed to have nothing more to do with the rebels because he realised how much distress and worry he was causing his parents.

He was the only one in the family who was outspoken in his support of the revolution. And he spent many hours with me explaining his viewpoint.

The Shah had not started out so badly, he said, when the British had propped him up on the throne in place of his father, Reza Shah, after the Second World War. But as his reign went on he became ever more of a megalomaniac, his dream to make Iran the third world power after the United

States and the Soviet Union. To this end he built up an incredible stockpile of weaponry with the vast revenues from oil which, wisely used, could have brought the country out of its Third World state.

His 'White Revolution' of the 1960s, an attempt to modernise Iran on Western models, was an exercise in image-building for the rest of the world. If anything, it impeded Iran's progress by introducing ambitious ill-conceived schemes that simply did not work.

The Shah's family and close supporters were notoriously corrupt, using their influence to build up vast personal fortunes. To maintain this hated regime it was necessary for the Shah to create the despised Savak, which infiltrated every level of society.

The Shah had also offended the large conservative religious majority by such moves as continuing the ban on the chadour that had been introduced by his father, and degrading the status of the religious seminaries as educational establishments. It was feared that he would turn the country into the kind of secular society that existed in the West, aspects of which many Iranians found contemptible. Under the Shah, Iran's politics were greatly influenced by the US, for its strategic importance was immeasurable.

I had never felt the slightest stirring of interest in politics, but as Mehdi spoke, drawing on metaphor after metaphor to make his argument come alive, I became absorbed in the story.

Eventually the Shah had to go. Everybody wanted to be rid of him, except those who were benefiting from the corruption and greed of the royal enterprise. Even the Americans wanted him gone, for he had learned well how to play politics and held a valuable bargaining tool in the threat of transferring his patronage to Russia.

At this point the main contestors to fill the power gap were the communist party and the religious party with its greatly respected leader, Khomeyni. He had been exiled many years earlier by the Shah for his outspoken criticism of the regime.

The countries of the West egged on the revolution behind the scenes, and clandestinely but effectively supported Khomeyni's return to Iran. He would suit their purpose well: pious, unskilled in the game, a blind man in the murky alleys of international politics, and a respected leader in a nation of great wealth and significance on the world stage. But of most importance was the expectation that he would effectively neutralise the threat of a communist takeover. What a surprise then when the ungrateful man refused all overtures from the United States – and the Soviet Union!

At last, Iran was to be free of all foreign influence. It was going to work out its own destiny on the path of the pure message of Islam. In this way it would avoid the corruption and dissolution, the moral degradation that seemed to be spreading throughout the world.

If the measures to achieve this were harsh and authoritarian, they were justified, Mehdi asserted. For what needed to be done could not be achieved through the democratic process. Under an incorruptible leader whose highly disciplined and godly life was totally given over to his task of totally reinstating the Shiah faith in its purity on one part of the globe, Iran would go forward as the model of a just society for the rest of the world, especially for those countries where the force of Islam had weakened and all but disappeared.

Mehdi brought me volumes painstakingly recreated from the papers urgently shredded by the American embassy staff so that they could never be used as evidence of political manipulation. They revealed a depth of US involvement far beyond what we had all been led to believe.

I began to understand the angry murals on the streets shrieking their hatred of Uncle Sam, the Russian bear, the Shah. I began to identify with this desire, strongly expressed by so many, that Iran be left alone to work out its own problems, to utilise its oil wealth as it saw fit, to be free at long last from all foreign interference.

Through these long discussions with Mehdi I came to realise that oil had been a mixed blessing for Iran. As the industrial nations became ever more dependent on oil, their interest in controlling events in the oil-rich countries became ever more pressing. Oil had brought Iran many problems as well as great wealth.

My country was no threat to Iran. This alone is why I could be wholeheartedly accepted, and allowed to feel the warmth of these people, who to the rest of the world appeared vengeful, violent, fanatical.

The Mujaheddin (holy warriors), highly trained guerrillas, ruthless in their pursuit of justice and freedom in their country, may have approached Mehdi to join forces in correcting what they saw as the excesses of the post-revolution regime. But even if he had agreed with their views, Mehdi's fighting days were over. Now a family man, he had enough problems meeting his own commitments and helping his patients, many of whom were the shattered victims of the war. Mehdi declined to be involved. He heard later, through a cousin who had visited Germany and been in touch with the Mujaheddin there, that it had been decided that Mehdi would not be punished. He was regarded well by the rebels for the good work he was doing in his own surgical practice and in Iran's teaching hospitals. He was luckier than some of his colleagues. Two other doctors he knew practising in Mashad were brutally murdered after declining to support the Mujaheddin.

CHAPTER 12

A COUNTRY AT WAR

I had arrived in a country at war, and still recovering from a bloody revolution the significance of which would become apparent only later with the amazing spread of fundamentalist Islam throughout the world. From my distant home I had imagined that everything would be put on hold until such a state of emergency had returned to normal. I had expected a terrible waiting, a collective holding of breath, but that is not what I found. Life went on, babies were born, weddings were planned, meals were cooked and shared, though all done with a certain resignation of the spirit.

Nevertheless, the war was never out of mind, though the front was far from us physically, on the opposite corner of the country. We were not actively defending the revolution, giving our lives into the hands of Allah each day with a prayer for martyrdom, but we were constantly reminded of the sacrifice that was being made on our behalves. Frivolity was considered irreverent and inappropriate. If you seemed to be enjoying yourself in a public place such as a restaurant, people would look at you with disapproval.

For some of the younger generation, cynicism was the mood. Unable to comprehend why the West was willing to provide arms to a madman, Iraq's Saddam Hussein, for a war that had no justification, they concluded that this was just another international plot to weaken both Iran and Iraq, to keep both countries locked in a mutually destructive conflict.

Reminders of the revolution and the holy war, the jihad, were everywhere. Huge posters and garish murals depicted the glory of war and martyrdom, the triumph of the faithful over the satanic forces of Iran's enemies. The water in one of Mashad's elegant fountains ran red symbolising the blood of the martyrs, both those who had sacrificed their lives during the overthrow of the Shah's regime, and those who were dying in the war with Iraq.

There was always a sense of being watched. The eyes of Khomeyni, made piercing by the iron will behind them, and those of his more fatherly religious colleagues, looked down from gigantic portraits painted on street walls and buildings. In the most unlikely nooks and crannies of offices, shops and homes one would come upon a photograph of the Imam, as he was respectfully called.

The pasdaran, the civilian guardians of the revolution, were also ever watchful. It was their duty to enforce the rules of Islam, especially as they applied under the present conditions. They patrolled the streets in groups on foot or in their tank-like vehicles, stopping civilians as they saw fit. Many of them were young men, into whose hands the regime had placed guns and, with them, power. Remembering our little 'adventure' at the checkpoint on the way from Tehran to Mashad I became very tense whenever I saw a power-struck teenager imposing his will upon another person, demanding identification papers, searching a car, questioning. I was told that if the pasdaran found the person suspect, or resistant, he could be taken to the komiteh. There he would be charged and probably punished on the spot.

Serious moral crimes included the use of alcohol and drugs, games of chance and gambling in any form (except, strangely, horse racing), prostitution, and being unchaperoned in the company of a member of the opposite sex who was not of one's immediate family. Homosexuality and adultery, which required four witnesses to sustain a charge, carried the death sentence. Of less importance but still evidence of anti-Islamic sentiment were activities such as playing any music except early classical, martial or religious music. And dancing, which was seen as an overt sexual activity.

The dress code applied to both sexes. Men were required to wear long sleeves and long trousers that were not too close-fitting. Open-necked shirts and beards acted as a sort of demonstration of allegiance to Islam. Women were not penalised for going without the chadour as long as the hair was totally covered, the body outline disguised under a long loose coat, and the legs made innocuous, in slacks, thick dark stockings or high boots. I personally found the chadour more comfortable, especially in summer.

Many ordinary citizens felt it their self-appointed duty to be the eyes and ears of the revolution. Occasionally a woman would startle me in the street by hissing vehemently at me, passing so close that I would feel her breath on my face. At first I did not know why – I felt that perhaps it was simply because I had been identified as a foreigner – but later I came to realise that it was because a wisp of hair had escaped from under my chadour or ruhsari.

Once when I was visiting Haram I found myself being followed by a vigilant Muslim woman who had identified me as foreign even though I was totally swathed in black like every other woman. My heart started to pound in my chest when I suddenly realised that guards had been summoned and an angry looking crowd was forming. The woman challenged me, asking me what I was doing in this place forbidden to all but Muslims. Fortunately I had by now enough Farsi to explain, in a rather shaky voice, that I was Muslim, married to an Iranian and from New Zealand. Then, miraculously, the crowd started looking at me with a different sort of interest and one woman asked me how I found their country. Had I been American, I doubt that they would have responded in the same way. Even as an Englishwoman I may have been unpopular, for the Iranians have long memories and they have not forgotten the Anglo-Iranian Oil Company and its exploitation of Iran's oil.

You could never escape the eyes of the dead. From shrines and the windows of their family home, from mosques and komiteh offices, lining the street walls, and from shop fronts, faces of young men looked out on the mundane lives of those left behind, and questioned them. Are you doing your duty, as I did mine? Are you submitting to God's will, as I did?

Two days each week, Shambe and Panj-shambe, the equivalent of our Saturday and Thursday, Mashad would prepare for the funeral of her martyrs. Ambulances would meet the army aircraft that had flown the bodies from the war zone and brought them to a central mosque, where families and mullahs would meet to begin the procession. The shops on the main street leading to Haram would be closed, the shutters pulled down and the street blocked to traffic. Sometimes the procession of mourners bearing coffins was short but other times, following an intense period of fighting, it seemed to go on for hours, with many coffins. The streets were lined with onlookers and echoed with the footsteps and chanting voices of thousands as this great wave of humanity made its way towards the holy place.

As each group arrived, the families of the martyrs seated themselves in one of the paved courtyards, spreading carpets to sit on and erecting a framed photograph of the dead man. The mullahs prayed and the women sobbed, their bodies heaving under their enveloping coverings. On my first occasion, as a bystander at the funeral of an unknown boy, I felt all the agony of losing Paulo come flooding back and I too turned away sobbing. But Mamajan took my face in her hands and admonished me with a stern 'Na kon!' From that day on I kept my sorrow hidden away. There was no place for self-pity in Iran.

Traditionally the mourning family provided fruit, sweets and coins, which they gave away to passers-by, requesting in return a prayer for the departed. The beggars from the nearby streets would desert their usual posts and follow the processions into the courtyards, knowing that donations of money and food would be forthcoming.

Each coffin was carried once around the outside circle of Haram, before being taken in through the maze of courtyards and internal corridors to the tomb of Imam Reza for a final blessing. Throngs of pilgrims made way for the black-clothed bearers, who chanted as they ran.

Family and coffin would later take their last journey together to the cemetery, where the body would be buried in the white shroud of the pure martyr.

In the main cemetery of Mashad, Behheshte Reza, great tracts of land had been put aside for the martyrs, and the empty, waiting space seemed to demand to be filled. Each martyr (shahid) had a small plot upon which stood his shrine, with a glass-enclosed placard showing the martyr in life and, where possible, in death, with a short account of his life, and a prayer for his resurrection in Allah's paradise.

Some of the faces appeared very young, and I wondered what this young person had known of life, death and glory when he chose his destiny.

There was a hush about the place, as there is in any cemetery, but here it was different. Even in the midst of the keening of mourning women there was a sense of stillness and expansion, as if one had stepped into another dimension. I felt that I had entered the heart of the martyr, which, even in the heat and terror of battle, carried a still silent faith, trusting that all was encompassed by the will of Allah.

A 'shahid zen deh' was a living martyr, one who had not lost his life but may have lost his sanity, or suffered terrible physical disability. Even though the government provided generous recompense, these men perhaps paid the highest price of all, with their torn and anguished bodies and dislocated sense of reality.

CHAPTER 13

FINDING A HUSBAND FOR SORAYA

One day I opened the heavy courtyard gate to put some items in my little white car, in preparation for a shopping expedition. I started at the sight that met my eyes. Like a trail of ducklings following mother duck, a line of eight black-chadoured women passed me, intent on their destination at the end of the alley. I wondered if someone in the neighbour's home had died. All but two of the women completely ignored me, so intent were they on their mission. The couple who did turn to me stared coldly, their eyes hard with disapproval, perhaps because my hair was uncovered and I wore jeans. I hurried inside, wanting to warn Mamajan, for the entourage seemed to be heading for her door. Soraya answered the phone.

'Soraya, a large group of women seem to be going to your place. Is everything all right?'

'No, it's not, Anna.' Her voice softened to a pleading tone. 'Please come over and help me. They are considering me as a bride for their relative. I hate this,' she said emphatically. 'Please come. Oh, they're here now. Come!' she commanded and hung up the phone.

I knew that Soraya was very worried at the prospect of having to choose a husband from among the men presented to her as suitable. She wanted to fall in love, she had told me, as I had fallen in love with Bijan; as her elder sister Nadia had fallen in love with Daniel while they were students. She had come to me very distressed the day her mother had spelled it out. The universities were closed and no-one knew when they would re-open. And even if she went to university she would not be allowed to mix with the men. There was no way she could meet a man except through an arrangement set up by the network of friends and relatives. And at 18 she certainly should be beginning to look for a partner she could come to love in time.

She had repeated her mother's words to me, sobbing. She knew there was no other way. But she hoped that among the men presented there would be one that she could at least like.

I remembered the day I had driven Soraya to the bazaar, when a terrific downpour had flooded the streets while we were shopping. We came out to find the little car sitting in several inches of water and, worse still, it wouldn't start. A young man had offered to push the car to get it going and then had followed us in his car to see that we got home safely. He was good-looking and I remember how Soraya had watched him out of the back window while he was pushing our car, his eyes on her. I felt for both of them, remembering the excitement of a mild flirtation when I was their age. They were so aware of each other's presence yet dared not exchange a word, and Soraya shook her head when I suggested we should invite him in for a hot drink, seeing he had been so kind to us and got his trousers wet into the bargain. She said she would have liked to see him again if it had been possible, but it simply was not possible.

The first time I had met one of Soraya's cousins at a family gathering I had asked her to point out her husband to me. She did so with a resigned look, and confessed that she didn't like him – he was old, and dull. But he had a good job so she had consented to marry him. Now she wished she had refused. I hoped this would not be Soraya's fate.

The tradition of arranged marriages, where children were betrothed at a very young age, no longer existed in Iran. It had been replaced by a more subtle version where selection was made on the basis of the status and wealth of the families involved, and the individuals' education and reputation. Although the final choice rested with the young people (and it was supposed to be the duty of the mullah who officiated at the marriage to ensure there was no coercion), it was inevitably based on superficial knowledge of each other, and often the overriding need for a home and a life of their own.

I did not want to get involved in family politics but, never having been to one of these gatherings before, I was curious and quickly made up my mind to join them. I donned my scarf and went next door.

Letting myself into the house, I heard voices coming from the drawing-room. This room, its ornate formal furniture normally shrouded in white sheets and its Persian carpets rolled up against the walls, was usually dark and deserted. Being the only furnished room in the house it was reserved for important occasions such as today's. This was the first time Mamajan had entertained in the room since I had been in Mashad. I understood that this meeting was a serious matter and I must be on my best behaviour.

I was nearly bowled over by Soraya as I entered the house. Rolling her eyes and pulling a face, she kissed me, whispering her thanks. Leading me into the occupied room she adopted a sweet innocent smile and, holding my hand, took me around to introduce me to each woman in turn. The women looked up at me with curiosity and surprise. A foreign wife in the family would add considerably to its esteem.

Dropping my scarf around my shoulders to show off my envied blonde hair I took a seat near Mamajan, who explained to the women that I was Bijan's fiancée, soon to be formally married. Dressed as I was in trousers, a sweater and stockinged feet, I was rather out of place in the formal gathering. Each woman had carefully selected her outfit and matching shoes, which had not been removed upon entering the house, as is the usual custom. They all wore jewels – not too many, not too few, just enough to establish wealth and good taste combined. Mamajan, uncharacteristically, wore a triple string of pearls and a large emerald ring to complement her simple classical dress. Soraya wore turquoise, less expensive and therefore more appropriate for a young unmarried woman.

The women were surprised to find that I spoke rudimentary Farsi and, with this discovery, quickly made me the centre of attention. Poor Soraya seemed to go hardly noticed as she went about her duty of handing out tiny glasses of tea in gold holders to the guests. Obviously nervous, being effectively on trial, she knew that despite their apparent attention elsewhere, these women were assessing her looks, her posture, her manners, her skills. Could she pour a dozen glasses of tea from the samovar, making sure each one was the right strength? Were the biscuits, which she had made and was now graciously handing about, delicious and delicate as they should be? Did she know how to groom herself to appeal to mother, sister, aunt and, above all, the absent male, who, if positively advised by these women, might propose?

The women sat, large in the expanse of their chadours, which, now loosened from their heads, billowed around their waists. They looked down their noses, as if they really believed in their authority to influence Soraya's future. Like petty officials who cling greedily to their small authority, they were ridiculous in their pomposity. Mamajan and I had already exchanged private looks, agreeing silently that we would not let Soraya marry into this brood however good the social prospects.

A wad of photographs was produced by the mother. The photos of the young man in question showed a reddish-haired, big-eared fellow in his twenties. We were informed by his proud mother that … yes, indeed, he was quite fair, almost like a European really. What's more, he was an engineer, with good prospects. Mamajan, in a rare show of one-up-manship, asked where he had trained. The reply was a little mumbled.

'Oh, ah, here, at the University of Mashad.' The prospective mother-in-law obviously knew that two of Mamajan's five children had received education abroad. Another point in our favour.

Now the tables had turned! The visitors, knowing themselves to be holding the losing hand, were desperately trying to sell the boy to us. Soraya, her own qualities enhanced by her family's success, was an exceptionally good catch, and enough subtle hints had been dropped for everyone to know that. Her fears allayed, Soraya had by now relaxed, relinquishing all social show, and was enjoying a cup of tea and eating more than enough tiny biscuits.

Before leaving the mother deposited three of the best photos of the potential groom on Soraya's lap, for her to brood over. It was agreed that Mamajan would contact her the following week with Soraya's decision.

Zoghra, the servant, joined us as we fell about giggling when the door was safely closed behind the group, while Mamajan, a devastating mimic, began imitating them, with their snobbish looks and sideways glances.

'He's definitely not the man for me!' Soraya exclaimed gleefully, ripping the photos in half.

CHAPTER 14

CAN I SURVIVE HERE?

Fehri was a strange little dark-skinned man who looked more Arabic than Iranian. He was passionately intense, so much so that few people took the time to get to know him properly. I was quite glad to see him again for we had first met in England. I recalled that nasal voice, as fluent in English as in Farsi, stopping for no-one but rattling on with a relentless flow of information, ideas, opinions. I remembered how his need for attention, and his passion to know more than anyone else, had driven me away initially. He never listened to anything that I, or anyone else, had to say. However, he did have a brilliant mind so in spite of myself I became a voyeur into the world of his thoughts, where drama and mystery were woven into enthralling stories.

He told us the story of his father, whose stature came not from an insistent loud voice but from scientific genius. He became a highly respected inventor, accumulating great wealth. In true storybook style he chose not to bank the proceeds from his successful enterprises, but kept the cash stashed in a secret place behind one of the wall panels in his home. As the mini-mountain of wealth grew he became ever meaner – not with his children, whose every whim was satisfied, but with his fourth wife, an ambitious young woman who had married him for his riches.

When the old man died mysteriously three years earlier, the young widow disappeared into the custody of her own family. The money also disappeared. The children strongly suspected that their father had been murdered but in that time of upheaval, civil turbulence and war, in which so many families lost loved ones, Fehri and his brothers and sisters could find no-one to investigate the accusation.

Fehri was haunted by his suspicions and his anger. He mourned the loss of his father and his inheritance. Living in the old family home he was constantly reminded of the tragedy, and his bitterness had made him shrink and shrivel until he became smaller, even smaller than I remembered him.

One evening, having shown us, and expounded upon, a fine collection of miniatures left him by his father, and entertained us with many exaggerated stories and a meal prepared by his father's old retainer, Fehri led us out into the night to see us on our way. We passed through the courtyard and the once magnificent garden of his paternal home. Now neglected and overgrown, it was reverting to wilderness, as were the dead man's children without his guiding hand.

Fehri kissed us goodbye with a passion true to his nature and wrung from us a promise that we would visit him again soon. I felt we were abandoning him to his sad memories as we drove away from the small, lonely, waving figure.

I turned to face the road ahead. Suddenly shots rang out in the night. One, two, three, four, five. My heart seized – my first thought was for Fehri. I looked back. His figure moved slowly towards the high gates of his home, his head bowed, seemingly deep in thought, as if he had not noticed the shots.

'That wasn't Fehri.' Bijan took my hand as he drove. 'Those shots came from the prison over there.'

He motioned towards a wall beyond Fehri's house. 'Fehri says that every night from midnight on they execute prisoners. He sometimes hears up to 50 shots in one night.'

The air stuck in my throat. My fingers clenched around Bijan's hand. I was well aware that executions took place in Iran, the fact was publicised. The victims could be traitors, or criminals, or those who had seriously transgressed the moral code. Until now it had always been happening somewhere far enough removed that though I could question it, abhor it, I somehow learned to live with it. But now here it was, so near, the unwelcome knowledge forced upon me in the dark night.

Something in me snapped. For the first time I was brought face to face with – what? Fear for myself, fear of the death I would one day have to face? Or was it the recognition of the violence of the society of which I was now a part?

Death. Death. Death. Life, so fragile, was surrounded by death, insistent and growing ever more palpable about us. Was my life, precious and purposeful to me, without value in the looming shadow of death?

Every day my ears heard the word death. Every day death was discussed in my presence. Every day the news of death came into my life.

A doctor, a colleague of Daniel's, homosexual was murdered, his throat slashed as he prepared to leave his clinic one night. The Mujaheddin, fighting to overthrow the Islamic regime, were blamed.

Muffled shots in the depth of night would be followed in the morning by proud proclamations, in the papers and over the loudspeakers, of a Muslim's moral duty done for the cause of Islam.

A martyr's shrine appeared outside our neighbour's house, commemorating the death of their 18-year-old son in the war. So often when I went up to the shops at the roundabout, there would be a new photograph on the walls – a new martyr, a new name on everyone's lips.

Revolution, war, death. I began to wonder how much more I could stand. Perhaps, I thought, it was easier for the Muslims with their faith in heaven and hell, in rewards for their pain and punishment for their wrongdoings, in an all-knowing God who understood what we mortals could never understand.

As autumn deepened into winter I became ill. I was unable to leave the house and my physical isolation symbolised the melancholy loneliness I now often experienced. Three months had taken their toll. I was alone with my mirror of snow lying all about me. I faced myself in its silence.

I was frightened by the knowledge that I had chosen to live in a place where cruel and brutal acts took place every day, where so much effort was needed to counter the poverty and the dust, and so many traps governed my life. Why was I passing my days in this strange country that was not my country? I had come to Iran full of curiosity, prepared to love the country and its people. But at this point I began to wonder if I could go on accepting, absorbing, so much that pulled my spirits down. I was also becoming aware that the smallest gap in my relationship with Bijan showed up my complete dependence on him, and my vulnerability.

I did not feel myself strong enough to battle against the insanity. I knew that I had to find some way to protect myself, as a prisoner must find a way to survive in his prison cell. The reality of his situation can drive him to despair unless he takes responsibility for creating his own life within the restricted world that he inhabits. Iran demanded no less of me. I needed to create my own life within the restricted world that I inhabited.

I saw that I could do this within my own home, and I began to do so. I learned to people my solitude and surround myself with those activities that kept my energy up, and avoid those that drained me. I was lucky to be able to borrow books in English of poetry, history and literature from the library at the University of Mashad, through a relative of Bijan's, who had been a lecturer in English literature there before it had been closed. I began painting lessons and set up my easel in a corner of our sitting-room to practise the techniques I was learning. Bijan framed my pictures and hung them on the wall. I had brought lots of cassette tapes from New Zealand, so the little apartment always rang with a great variety of music. I sewed some comfortable but rather exotic clothes to wear about the house. I charged the atmosphere around me with vibrancy and colour.

Our few good friends congregated regularly in our home, and were always welcome. But before long too many wanted to share the little haven of beauty and sanity that we had created. My refuge was invaded and my inspiration began to die in the face of duty. Playing the Persian hostess was not a role I found rewarding. Yet I could not ask Bijan to change his ways, the way of his culture, where every visitor at your gate is seen as a gift from God. This sounds poetic and in theory is a good philosophy, but I, seeking space, found the expectations of Persian hospitality unbearably demanding.

I needed to protect myself also from the tales of suffering and tragedy that visitors to my home brought. Often I would meet someone at the door and immediately be hit by a wave of emotion – sadness, anger, frustration.

Only much later I learned that my experience of that emotion was my ability to act as a channel for unexpressed feelings in others. At first this experience baffled and concerned me, for there were certain people in whose presence I became utterly off-balance and clumsy, dropping crockery and glassware, tripping over the step, flustered and unable to function in a normal way.

During this time I became familiar with the work of the Sufi poets, Sa'di, Rumi, Khayyam and others who used the symbolic language of love and wine to express love of the divine. There was also the great epic *Shahnameh, the Book of Kings*, which recounts the stories of this Aryan race from its earliest mythical origins, in the manner of Homer's *Iliad*. It was written a thousand years ago by Ferdousi in the language of the Persians, at a time when most of the population had adopted Arabic, the language of their Islamic conquerors.

The *Shahnameh* provided the impetus for the resurgence of Farsi as a literary vehicle, and of pride in the ancient Zoroastrian religion and culture, all of which had been driven underground in preceding centuries. Ferdousi defined the Iranian personality as distinct from the Arabic and saved the Persian language from extinction. Since that time it has flourished, though it still retains the Arabic alphabet and many Arabic borrowings.

I realised that I had always tended to think of Iranians as closely related to Arabs and Jews, the Semitic races, and was surprised to learn that they, with Indians, are from the same stock as Europeans. Their language, developed from the same root as Latin, Greek and the Germanic languages, has many similarities to English. Hitler used the term Aryan in a very narrow sense, to describe the fair-skinned, fair-haired races of Northern Europe, but it actually applies to a very much wider racial group.

Poetry is one of the great loves of the Persians, and a popular pastime is spontaneous versifying. The first time I was present at one of these occasions I did not realise that the poet was improvising as he went along, so racy and unfaltering was the metre. Even I could hear the rhymes, though I hardly understood the words. He was standing in the middle of the room, declaiming his lines in a theatrical voice, waving his arms dramatically and changing his facial expressions to suit the context, while everyone clapped or beat out the rhythm with him. The conclusion was greeted with cheers and congratulations.

Before we had left Tehran, Bijan and I had visited one of the few remaining bookshops in the city, where I was shocked to discover not one title in English.

However, the visit was not in vain for I was served by a young man who brought a large book and placed it in my hands, shouting in his clumsy English, 'Get your husband to translate this to you.'

It was the *Masnavi* of Mevlana, a name that meant nothing to me until I discovered later that this was an alternative name for the poet Rumi, whose work was familiar to me.

The shop assistant was gesturing wildly to get our attention. Extending both hands before him he said with great intensity, as if sharing a secret with me, 'You put all the books of the world in this hand,' he lowered his left hand, 'and then you put the *Masnavi* in this hand,' allowing his right hand to sink to the floor, 'and it is this one that is heavier! This is the greatest book ever written.' He grinned broadly for he had found a way to make his point.

This had been my introduction to an aspect of Iran of which I was totally ignorant: the tradition of Sufism, a tradition that has survived and diversified since the earliest years as the mystical or esoteric arm of Islam. One day in the street I saw a strangely dressed man wearing a sort of bowler hat and carrying a bowl and a bell. I was told he was a Sufi who belonged to a certain religious order of dervishes. He had no home and lived on charity.

I had often heard Bijan and his friends speak of someone as a dervish and I was interested to meet one. Karim, who lived on the outskirts of Mashad, qualified, for he had chosen to live a simple unworldly life as a renunciate, which gave him time to study the works of the great philosophers of his religion, and to find the ecstasy of divine communion by playing the santour and meditating. He studied under the great Sufi teachers who travelled throughout the country.

The religious establishment may have seen Sufis as self-indulgent in their focus on self rather than society. But it really had nothing against them, for though they chose to pray and fast in private rather than observe the out-

A carpet bazaar in the north east. The men wear high karacul hats, the women colourful shawls. (*Photo: N. Kasraian*)

The golden dome of the shrine of Imam Reza, Mashad. *(Photo: N. Kasraian)*

A Qashgai woman in a tribal camp near Persepolis. (*Photo: N. Kasraian*)

Entrance to Isfahan's Imam Mosque, which was built in 1641 during the reign of Shah Abbas. (*Photo: N. Kasraian*)

ward rituals of Islam, they were Muslims in the purest sense, interested in the essence of Islam, the philosophy rather than the form. The personal life lived with integrity, rather than the outer social and political environment, was their concern. I found the dervishes to be the most creative and personally integrated of all the Muslims I met. Their goal was not to pay homage to any long-dead system of beliefs, but to discover the truth in their own experience and their own life.

I had been interested in Hinduism and Buddhism, and found the Islam of the Sufis held a much greater appeal for me than the orthodox form. I looked to experience the meaning of 'god' myself through meditation, not through an outward show of worship. Perhaps this was why I was drawn so strongly to Bijan, who had a lot of the dervish in him. He never talked much about his beliefs, or claimed any religious superiority. But I could understand why his friends jokingly called him a dervish. Many of his qualities had drawn me to him: his good looks, his courage, his gentleness and generosity, his intelligence. But there was also this recognition of his potential for spiritual growth, something deeper than his other qualities, something that called to my own nature.

One aspect of my study of the esoteric side of Islam was my interest in the character of Ayatollah Khomeyni. In conversation with trusted friends I tried to find out as much as I could about him. In the West he was, and still is, portrayed in strongly negative terms. It was bearing this influence that I came to Iran, to experience the results of the work of this man.

His uncompromising integrity and open opposition to the Shah had been the catalyst for freeing the country from 25 centuries of mostly oppressive monarchical rule. True enough, those haunting eyes, which watched us wherever we went, seemed to stand in harsh judgment of us ordinary weak humans. Yet was the power he wielded simply based on fear? Fear of the hellfire of the Koran, or of the more immediate hell that awaited anyone breaching its injunctions? I could not believe that fear was the only source of his power. I believe it lay more in the enormous respect for him shown by much, if not all, of the nation. This was no ordinary dictator, seeking power for his own ends. His life was utterly given over to serving his God, to carrying out

God's plan as he understood it to be. We could disagree with his interpretation of that plan. However, we should try to see in him not a cruel autocrat, but an extreme example of the piety and simplicity of the truly religious man.

My need to comprehend the true phenomenon of Ayatollah Khomeyni, rather than the cliché the West had pinned onto him, was founded in my need to understand the fundamentalist movement of Islam if I were to remain in Iran. Otherwise my time here would be like a prison sentence, during which I took what pleasure I could from life, but longed for a change in my circumstances.

CHAPTER 15

GOLSARA, PLACE OF FLOWERS

As spring began to thaw the earth and bring the first stirrings of renewed life in my garden, we prepared to travel south to visit friends at their family estate. Golsara, meaning place of flowers, was a small village on a wide plain edged by mountains that kept their snow for much of the year. It was most beautiful in the 'bright' season, our friends told us, when the desert flowers began to push their way through the cold soil.

We arranged to meet Nasser and his brother, Ali, at the village one Thursday evening, early in spring. The night was all around us as we left Mashad and the last snow of winter lay thinning on the ground. The full moon lit our way over the unfamiliar road, gilding the patches of snow on either side. Riding high in the big white jeep, I let my ruhsari fall around my shoulders and, shaking my hair free, was surprised to find that I felt very daring and exposed, I had become so used to covering my hair. The freedom was exhilarating. Behind us lay the claustrophobia of the city, with all its uniformed guards, guns, graffiti, propaganda, rules and regulations. Before us, somewhere in the darkness, was Golsara.

I was always so aware of being a foreigner in the Iranian culture. But here I was no more an alien in the wilderness that lay all around us than any other human who ventured out into these surroundings.

Laughing, chatting, dozing, shivering, in love with the adventure, we sped across the plains, passing occasionally through a huddled cluster of buildings, ghostly sleeping hamlets lit only by the moon.

At one point an inexplicable shape looming near the side of the road turned out to be a shepherd in traditional garb. I could make out a head in a fitting hat, and below it a huge square coat, a garment made of thick layers of felt, resting on a stick across the shepherd's shoulders. This provided a sort of tent that protected the lonely man's body against the cold and propped him up so that he could sleep upright.

We drove for hours until the track petered out altogether and we knew we had gone wrong somewhere. So it was back to the nearest town where, luckily for us, an attendant was still in the petrol station, though it must have been nearly midnight. We learned from him that there are two villages called Golsara separated by a low mountain range. We were by now desperate to get there, so we set off along the other side of the range.

No sign except a straggling line of trees marked the bumpy, barely distinguishable track to the second village of Golsara. Ahead, the mounds that signified dwellings were outlined against the sky. Typically, the directions to the particular house we sought in the village had been sketchy, requiring us to use whatever imagination and intuition we could muster at that late hour. In this case we were searching for the first tower on our left! As we turned down a little track between adobe houses, the tower stood before us. Three times the height of the other buildings, and narrowing towards the top, its shape was echoed by another such tower far off to the right, suggesting that this had once been a walled village, although there was no sign now of the connecting wall.

The moonlight glinted off puddles of ice in the potholed road as we climbed down from the truck and approached a large wooden gate set in a stone wall beside the tower. Bijan grasped a big metal ring in his cold hands and banged it to announce our arrival, but gently, for he was reluctant to disturb the whole community at this unusual hour. No response, except the barking of a dog. By the time we had been standing there, shivering, for 10 minutes, we were beginning to wonder whether we were at the right gate, the right tower – and even, after all our driving, the right village!

Eventually we heard a shuffle, then a key in the lock, and there before us stood the huddled, half-dressed figure of our friend Nasser, rubbing his eyes.

How relieved we were to see that familiar face. The kerosene lamp he carried threw long shadows across the cobbled courtyard, barren but for a few spindly trees. An arched doorway led straight into a large room, its floors lined with kilims, mattresses and sleeping bodies, for we were joining a weekend 'house party'. We gratefully crawled under the sheepskins on one unoccupied mattress. I lay awake for some time, listening to the soft breathing, and feeling the building, sensing the lives that had been lived here over the centuries.

The morning revealed our quarters in greater detail. The house, once quite grand and at least 200 years old, had belonged to Nasser's family for five generations. Now it was run down, its high mud-brick walls being gradually eaten away by the harsh seasons, its floor and ceilings bowing under the weight of the years. The doors and window frames, warped by the extremes in temperature, were ill-fitting, and the mosaic designs in the paved courtyard had faded and chipped. Nasser explained that there were no plans to renovate the house because the cost involved could not be justified. The brothers used it only irregularly as a retreat from the city, when they felt like some riding, hunting and simple living.

Nasser, apologising profusely that we should have spent our first night sleeping in the same room as his male guests, showed us up a stone staircase ascending the tower to a bedroom at the top: the best in the house, especially cleaned and prepared for us. A solid high oak bed, made up with fine linen, was generously covered with comfortable mattresses, sheepskins and woollen blankets. Obviously foreigners were thought to feel the cold! The room was otherwise bare except for a small wall mirror. Standing on tiptoes I could just see out of the high slit windows, pierced through two metres of packed, dried mud. The thick walls not only provided insulation from heat and cold, but in the past had provided some security from Turkman invaders. The village, frosty and deserted in the cold morning air, spread out below, dozens of little mud 'igloos' looking like small mounds from above.

Cheerful female servants, squatting on the kitchen's packed earth floor while they prepared breakfast, looked up at me inquisitively. They excitedly explained that it was the first time that anyone in the village could remember a European visiting Golsara, let alone a woman. The little community was all abuzz with the news and a special feast of welcome was already in preparation.

One of the servants, Maryam, invited me to come and watch her baking the bread for breakfast. Followed by a giggling throng of village girls, we made our way to a rough outhouse blackened by smoke and filled already with the smell of a fire. The hole in the ground, the oven, burned like a furnace and gave off intense heat when the lid covered with damp rags was lifted off. Maryam had her bread already rolled into portions of the right size which she skilfully pulled and threw, until each piece was stretched into a thin, oval-shaped sheet of dough the length of her arm. Leaning down into the oven, she threw the bread against the oven wall, causing it to stretch even more in its descent and stick to the wall. It emerged, fished out by a long hook, three minutes later, crisp and delicious. Maryam told me that she went through this process every morning, preparing the bread for the day, as bread was needed for every meal. The villagers ate much less rice than the city folk because it was now imported and cost more.

Golsara was a poor village. There was a village tap but no electricity or sewerage and only one bus a week to the nearest town. To have a bath the locals had to travel to the next village as there was no public hamam.[13] This was evidently typical of the majority of villages in Iran. Its inhabitants went about their seasonal rituals seemingly unaware of events in the wider world.

I asked Maryam if the revolution had changed her life. She replied without apparent bitterness.

'We are still waiting for the mullahs to come and place the money from the oil in our hands. This is what they promised us when the Shah left but it hasn't happened yet.'

Food, apart from the guaranteed rations from the government, was more expensive and less available. 'We mostly just eat what we grow in the village, and these days a bit more bread.'

Maryam's daughter, Fatima, showed me how she practised carpet weaving on the small portable loom her father had made. Her job was to provide prayer rugs for the villagers, so each day she squatted in the sun, threading and knotting, for several hours. She would soon learn to work the big loom. At 12 she needed to work towards perfecting the craft so that her father would get a good price for her when it was time to marry in two or three years.

She spoke with certainty that this was her destiny. No other possibility had been presented to her. She attended school sporadically, but her most important task was not to learn to read and write but to become experienced in running a home and making carpets. I marvelled at such willingness to go forward in life with no sense of choice, remembering the extensive and confusing array of options I had been faced with at Fatima's age. However, I felt I would only disturb her tranquillity by questioning her about her future.

As we walked through the village on a little tour we saw a number of boys and men hovering in front of the only 'shop'. They were squatting on their heels or leaning against a wall, joking, the men among them all smoking, as if to relieve their boredom, as they watched a goat being slaughtered. They grew silent and watchful as we passed, returning our 'salaam'. Nasser joked that it was obviously the women who did most of the work: baking the bread, helping to harvest the crops, preserving the precious meat in fat, weaving the carpets, and sewing the clothes on hand-turned machines. And I could see for myself that there would be a never-ending war against the mud from the unpaved streets and the open yards where the women cooked. Mud in the winter, dust in the summer.

I was aware of dark-clad forms slipping behind walls as we approached – the women trying to get a glimpse of me, the farangi, without being seen. The children were less discreet and followed us in increasing numbers at some distance, their eyes wide with wonder. When I turned to smile at them they turned away in embarrassment, but eventually some bold spirits returned my smile. When I felt I had their confidence I started playing a game with them. I would turn suddenly and raise my hands in claws and pull an ugly face, at which they shrieked and ran away, while I took a step or two after them. Of course they wanted more, but Nasser warned me against causing anyone to run within the village. The dogs might interpret it as a thief running away and give chase. So we resumed our sedate strolling, the children following expectantly, hoping for a bit more fun.

Surrounding the village was the land that would soon be ploughed for planting the crops. Beyond that stretched a great expanse of seemingly bare earth, where even now the flocks of sheep and goats foraged among the snowdrifts in the care of youthful shepherds. They were accompanied by dogs to protect them against the depredations of wolves. These huge dogs wore spiked collars to protect their throats from attack. I wondered whether the shepherds ever made pets of these animals, for I knew the Muslim attitude was that dogs were like pigs, unclean. Yet, in that lonely life, what comfort a friendly dog would have provided.

We were too early for the wild red tulips that were the symbol of martyrdom. We found only one during a long walk over the plains, but what a miracle it seemed, pushing up through the bare frozen earth.

Back at the house, in front of a roaring fire, the talk was as always of the past. I learned that it would have been unthinkable 30 years ago, when Iran was a feudal country, for the servants to share the house with the descendants of the landowner, or khan, which was now the situation for Nasser and Ali. The Shah's White Revolution of the mid-1960s had dispossessed the wealthy landowners of their property – huge tracts of land, including many villages and all their inhabitants. The land was turned over to the peasants who lived and worked there in a noble but unworkable gesture like many others made by the Shah in the cause of modernisation. According to Nasser, a horticulturist, it had helped no-one, causing productivity to decline and poverty in the villages to increase. The peasants lacked both organisational ability and the funds for equipment to enable them to utilise the land fully, as it had been when governed efficiently by a khan. They now existed on the produce of small plots and meagre flocks. They had little to sell, therefore little to spend on the scanty provisions available in the dusty grubby shed that served as a shop. Those who could provide a service, as the miller did with his huge grinding stones pulled by donkeys, were the lucky ones.

The brothers may not have spoken out against the present regime in any but the most trusted company but there was no longer any need to hide their contempt for the Shah. As landowners their harshest criticism was for the policies that made the country reliant on imports in return for oil and thus undermined its productivity, whereas it had once been self-sufficient. It sounded to me as if the country had been lurching from one disaster to another for a long time now.

At one point I brought up the subject of terrorist acts by Islamic fundamentalists in neighbouring countries. From listening to the television news in English, it had been hard for me to ascertain whether the government of Iran dissociated itself from them, encouraged them, or merely ignored them. I was concerned that they were alienating the outside world from Iran.

Nasser explained that, while he deplored the terrorism, he did understand why it was happening. He said the British with the backing of other Western powers were the ones who had created the problem in the first place by causing many thousands of Palestinians to be homeless. This situation was still there like an ulcer, refusing to be healed and poisoning relationships in the Middle East. But sadly there did not appear to be any financial gain for the West in solving the problem, though this was a very short-term view.

A very strong element in the Shiite faith was solidarity, Nasser explained, between all Muslims, not just Shiites, and the only way to stop the terrorism was to help the Palestinians in their battle for the right to a homeland. Israel had to give up its ambitions for territory. It must settle down and live in peace beside its Arab neighbours. Until the rest of the world understood this and made a commitment to bringing it about, the terrorists would continue to try to grab the world's attention and the terrorism would go on.

I could only hope that Nasser was right, and that the Palestinian 'problem' would soon capture international attention, and give peace in the Middle East a chance to develop.

We returned to Golsara several times in the coming months, to see the different phases of planting, tending and harvesting, to feel the wan warmth of the winter sun grow to its full scorching power in midsummer.

On one visit Nasser harnessed his young stallion, a little chestnut with a wild flash in his eye. He had not been exercised much over winter and his young body was bursting with pent-up energy. He pranced and twisted as Nasser threw a sheepskin and a soft handmade rug over his back, bound in place by a thick leather girth strap.

Bijan had proudly announced the night before that I was a good rider, for he knew that as children Matt, Lizzie, Paulo and I had each had our own pony. So it had been voted that I should exercise the horse today. What Bijan omitted to say was that I was not accustomed to riding half-wild stallions without the benefit of saddle, stirrups or hard hat!

I think Nasser's expectation was that he would lead me around the village a few times. But the horse, and I, had different plans. As I surveyed the dusty plain stretching for miles until it met the mountains I realised that if he got out of control I might just have to stay with him until he exhausted himself. Before mounting, I took the reins and spoke softly to him, stroking his nose and calming him, trying to calm my own thumping heart in the process. But suddenly, that special smell of horseflesh took me back – I was at home, grooming Tusitala, Paulo's pony, in preparation for the girl who was going to buy him to arrive and ride him away forever. We were standing in the horse paddock, under the great oak tree, its new spring leaves gently unfurling. I brushed away the coarse white winter hair to reveal underneath the shiny pale salmon of his new coat, marvelling once more at this annual transformation. The memory was so stark, so overpowering, that for a moment I had to hide my face in the stallion's mane before I could continue.

Nasser gave me a leg-up. As soon as the horse felt my weight he began to pig-jump in an attempt to dislodge me. I tried to hold him in but he started out across the plain, kicking up dust in swirls and clouds that made him start when he saw it out of the corner of his eye. I clung on with my knees and held his head firmly, willing him to feel my authority as he stretched his long legs over the ground.

A grove of trees clustered around a small stream ahead of us, and in the shade of the trees I could see some reclining figures, their heads turned towards our approach. Black and white goats, their heads bobbing up and down from where they drank, rattled their bells with each movement.

I managed to rein the horse in near the water, and let him drink a little from the stream. Golsara was a speck on the distant horizon, and a trail of dust marked the course we had followed.

I exchanged a few words with the astonished shepherds, who giggled at my uncovered blonde hair. I tried to delay the ride home until I had regained a little strength, as I knew that it would be even more hectic than the trip out. But with a mind and will of his own the horse, after a few pulls on the water, wheeled and took off at a gallop. Giving him free rein, I lay along his neck and relaxed into a feeling of exhilaration. I was a messenger flying in front of a foreign army. I heard the thud of hundreds of hooves. I was a scout scanning the territory before battle. The horse and I were one, lost in the past on this ancient plain.

Judging by the look of incredulity on their faces as we emerged from our dust cloud, I am certain that Nasser and his companions did not expect to see the horse and me arrive back together. He had never seen a woman ride a horse, let alone a wilful stallion. I reacted nonchalantly to the profuse compliments, secretly feeling extremely relieved that I had managed even to stay on the horse! However, I had struck a small blow for equality of the sexes, and basked in the new level of respect I was accorded.

One day, when several of Nasser's friends had come down for a weekend's shooting, we were taken on a picnic into the mountains. I rode my friend the stallion, of course, while the men walked with guns, hoping to shoot birds.

Not for the first time I was amazed at the amount of work Iranians were prepared to put into planning a picnic. It was not a matter of throwing a few things into the boot of a car and driving to some handy spot. In this country picnics were often major logistical enterprises, undertaken with great joy and anticipation, involving food preparation prior to departure, arranging donkeys to transport carpets, drinks, food in huge pots, sometimes even seats, to the remotest place one could find, preferably near running water and beneath the umbrellas of enormous shady trees.

In the act of laying down their carpets upon the earth, and building the fire to warm their food, the Persians seemed to proclaim the untamed place their own. Perhaps they did return that evening to a city lacking beauty, but a part of them remained out there, wandering beside the running water and reclining under the magnificent tree. They were not demonstrative or vocally appreciative, as I was, amazing them by hugging trees and exclaiming about the beauty of nature. Their communion was silent, and at first I doubted that it existed at all. But, as I saw the pains they went to in order to reach their destination, I understood that it was no less powerful an experience for them than for me.

It was about togetherness, about the family, the clan, moving as a single unit. So as we wandered up the river valley, the entire household from servants to horse trainer to donkey owners spread over quite a distance, all moving at their own pace. How cumbersome and slow it all seemed to me, who liked to make quick decisions and travel light. But I was learning about the nomadic heritage of these people and had to let go of my individualism and allow myself to be part of this group. In relaxing into it, I found a curious security. There was an unexpected power in being one of a tribe.

On our way we passed a small house standing alone, far from the village. Its owners turned out to be people from town who came here every summer. With typical Iranian hospitality they would have provided chai for everyone, but Nasser declined on our behalf, at which the woman ran to an apple tree, shook it vigorously and gathered up a bag of apples for us. Then she threw aside a pile of wet sacks and gave us drinks of icy cold water from a ceramic container kept cool by the sacks. As we left she threw water after us to safeguard our return. Compared with people like these 'ordinary' Iranians, we of the West simply do not know the meaning of hospitality.

We found our paradise in a grove of lime-green new-leafed trees, beside a meandering stream banked with mint. Fires were lit between stones and huge food pots balanced over the embers.

Appetites sharpened by the long trek made short work of the food, and then it was time for siesta and, for some, prayers. I fell fast asleep on my carpet, and woke to a cup of chai with a strangely different flavour. One of the manservants whose job it was to prepare the tea had found an aromatic herb growing near the creek and had added a handful, for the Iranians, especially the peasants, know the herbs that grow wild and use them with confidence.

It was a weary party that dined on bread and fetta cheese back at the village and reluctantly returned to civilisation that night, after promises to come again soon.

What magic times we had there! At the very name Golsara I feel my heart stir a little, and remember the smiling rugged faces of the peasants and the warmth of their greetings and farewells. I wonder, do they still remember the farangi?

CHAPTER 16

A VISIT TO THE ACADEMY OF BEAUTY

I had met Sogand only once, when she approached me with a favour to ask. She was a young woman of 19 completing a course as a make-up artist and for her final exam she had to demonstrate her skills at bridal make-up on a live model. I, the exotic foreigner, was asked to be that model.

She told me earnestly that she would come with her brother in his car to collect me on the morning of Chahrshambe, Thursday, three days hence, to take me to the Academy of Beauty. I insisted that I would meet her there as it was quite a pleasant walk from my home. Her tone was slightly apprehensive as she hung up the phone, doubtful that I would turn up but not wanting to be too pressing. I did, however, as arranged.

The young students and their raven-haired Iranian models gathered around me in the large first-floor room that constituted the beauty school. The students, excited and anxious before their exam, cast envious glances in Sogand's direction. Where had she found such a rare specimen? They stood around my chair before the mirror and stroked my blonde hair. Even the teacher gave me a warm welcome.

'Is that her natural hair colour?' whispered one of the students to the teacher, her face tense with disbelief, not realising that I understood Farsi.

Intrigued by the question herself, the teacher surreptitiously edged towards me and nonchalantly stroked my hair, lifting it up cautiously to examine the roots. She stood back proclaiming with great authority, 'Yes, it is her own colour.'

The girls gasped and began chattering among themselves, filled with the wonder of such a miracle of nature.

'What a colour!'

'How beautiful.'

'Imagine having hair like that.'

'Could I bleach mine to look like that?'

Sogand alone was silent, turning her head towards her make-up bag with a faint smile, while I coughed to hide my rising laughter. Neither of us wanted to disappoint them all by announcing the truth. Just six days ago I had visited the best hairdresser in Tehran to have my dark blonde hair frosted. I had walked out several hours later with a head of the most startling blonde hair. Upon questioning Fatimeh, the friend who had accompanied me to have her black roots touched up to blonde, I was unable to establish whether she had given the wrong instructions to the hairdresser, or whether frosting was simply an unknown technique in Iran.

While my revered hair dried in prickly curlers, Sogand began making me up, her hands massaging and smoothing a heavy, dark-toned foundation cream all over my face and neck as if to cover the bad skin I did not have. She concentrated her mind, her hands and all her knowledge on the small area of my upturned face, advancing slowly and painstakingly through all the stages of a traditional bridal make-up. Bright pink blusher on cheeks and temples, heavy blue eyeshadow ringing my green eyes, shiny black eyeliner, red lipstick outlined in brown pencil and finally the finishing touch. Out of their little plastic box and onto my eyelids, top and bottom, were put two pairs of thick black false eyelashes!

My back was towards the mirror as all this concentrated work took place, for I, as the bride, was not permitted to peep at myself during the entire procedure. Nor could I see what was happening to any of the other model-brides on either side of me, for Sogand was constantly busy with my face.

Not until the whole job was finished and my hair had been released from the uncomfortable curlers and arranged in elaborate curls under a heavy net of hairspray, was I permitted to see myself.

The sight that greeted my eyes shocked me into stunned silence. A painted mask covered my face, with only my buried eyes confirming that yes, this really was me. I felt like a witch or a doll, a prostitute desperate for a client, but to the women in the room I represented the pinnacle of bridal beauty.

All work in the room stopped and everyone held their breath as the teacher examined me from every angle. She wrote a list of numbers, obviously points given for the various aspects of the make-up job. She walked away towards an unused corner of the room as she tallied the list and then called a nervous Sogand to her side.

After a mumbled exchange, the now smiling Sogand came back to where I sat and threw her arms around me. 'Thank you, thank you. Full marks,' she whispered.

The teacher called after her. 'Your mark was so good only because your model is beautiful.'

My skin crawled under the make-up. I was itching to get it off. But first the photos had to be taken, dozens of them it seemed. Me alone, me with Sogand, me with the teacher, me with the whole class, me with some of the other models. I was truly the celebrity that day and every woman in the room wanted to look like me: fair-haired, fair-skinned, green-eyed, foreign.

Cold cream and warm water had never felt so good. A tail of oily, discoloured water ran down the plughole as I scrubbed my face clean, enthusiastically washing away Sogand's painstaking masterpiece. I swept my hair under my dark scarf and pulled on my long coat. Now I was the truly Islamic woman again, fit to be seen in public – anonymous, uniformed, colourless.

I chuckled to myself as I skipped down the stairs to the street, recalling the many times I had sat across a coffee table looking at the wedding album of my hostess for the day. It always took great imagination to affirm that the glamorous extravagant bride depicted in the endless photos was in fact the same woman as this anonymous, uniformed, colourless woman serving me coffee.

Such were the contrasts of life in this country of passionate martyrdom and exquisite artistry, this place of extremes. Seeming contradictions hid in many corners of Iranian life, and the paradoxes kept me guessing and searching, always intrigued, always surprised.

CHAPTER 17

OUR WEDDING

I had been in Iran nearly six months and my temporary marriage was about to become invalid. Should I stay and enter into a permanent marriage with Bijan? Or should I go?

There was never any doubt in my mind that Bijan and I belonged together. He could not leave Iran. His passport had been commandeered, and would be held until he turned 30 in nine months' time. This was the position for all males between the ages of 15 and 30. From this pool of young men the government could conscript for the armed forces, should the supply of willing martyrs ever dry up.

Meanwhile his business as a small paint manufacturer was doing well. He was working very hard at it, though there were at times difficult hold-ups in the supply of materials. But he was able to sell easily all that he made. The future in the short term looked reasonably secure.

Yet I did not feel that I would be happy to have children and bring them up in Iran under the present regime. Especially girls, for their lives are greatly restricted by religious conventions. A little girl is expected to start covering her hair before puberty, and after that time must have no contact with males other than family members. The poet Rumi expounded on the virtue of separate development by comparing men and women with fire and water. If there is no separation, water extinguishes the fire.

Two views of a wedding sofreh, each with the Koran displayed prominently at the centre.

LEFT: Anna dressed for her wedding.

BELOW: With Bijan, leading the wedding dance.

RIGHT: At the cherry orchard.

BELOW: Picking strawberries at the cherry orchard.

Nasser had never seen a woman ride a horse, let alone a young stallion.

Village men at Golsara wearing the ancient style Persian hats.

I thought of Bijan's little niece in Tehran, still young enough to enjoy riding her bicycle with her friends of both sexes in the quiet streets around her home, her dark hair flying out behind her. She would be nine next year. She would soon have to put away her bicycle, and remain indoors in a stuffy house during the warm summer evenings. She would have to forgo her tomboyish ways and learn to be docile and biddable, preparing herself for her destiny as wife and mother. This was not my wish for any daughter I might have.

The young woman's marriage will probably be arranged, or at least 'manipulated' if she is upper class, so that she marries someone suitably affluent and from a similar background. After marriage, the woman will normally play a secondary role, her areas of responsibility being the home and children. There will be no doubt as to who is the head of the household, and the husband's word is law. So marriage to a jealous or unreasonable husband could be hell. She will not presume to know about her husband's business in any detail, his successes or his failures, so she may never be aware of the financial strain she may be placing upon him by demands that seem normal to her. The husband will, if he is able, lavish jewels and expensive clothes on her, as the showpiece of his success. The canary in the gilded cage.

This typical situation was made very clear to me through a conversation I had with Bijan's friend Ali. When he and his wife had entertained us in their luxurious apartment, Homa had been dressed very expensively and loaded with gold. I was therefore surprised to learn that Ali wanted to buy a second-hand truck from Bijan but was unable to raise enough for the down-payment.

Some time later as we were walking together out of view of the villagers on the plain near Golsara and out of earshot of the rest of the party, I risked asking Ali how it was that he was having to pass up a good opportunity for lack of a quite small sum.

'I simply can't get hold of any cash, Anna. We're living on credit. I'm very worried. I don't know what the outcome will be.'

'What does Homa feel about this, Ali? Would she be prepared to cut expenses, perhaps even shift to a cheaper apartment?'

'I haven't spoken to her about it. I couldn't. She wouldn't understand. Women in Iran don't understand about business.'

'Yet you can speak to me about it, Ali.'

'It's different with you, Anna. Bijan can tell you his problems, I know he does, and you don't lose respect for him. But no man in Iran is respected if he goes around asking his wife for her opinion, telling her his business. She would tell her sisters and they would all laugh at me. I'm the head of the family, this is my business, nothing to do with her.'

'Yet, whatever you do, your decision is going to affect her.'

'She's my wife. I'll try to protect her from hardship, but if it comes to that she'll just have to put up with it.'

Women's rights, such as the right to inherit, or divorce, are addressed in the Koran, but they are not equal to the rights accorded to men. Nevertheless, there was always provision for caring for the woman and meeting her practical needs. A widow usually became the responsibility of her husband's brother. The divorced woman, however, was likely to find herself socially ostracised and, because she was no longer a virgin, have difficulty finding a second husband. A man could divorce his wife by repeating the words 'I divorce you' three times, while a woman had to prove that there were several unacceptable conditions, such as physical abuse, addiction to drugs or alcohol, or failure to consummate the marriage. The divorced woman would normally lose her children to the husband or his family.

In the past a married woman had to face the possibility of being displaced from first position by subsequent wives. Polygamy was still legal under Islamic law, but very much the exception in Iran. The husband had to prove that he could afford to support more than one wife. To quote the Koran: 'The Almighty said, "Marry of such women that please you: two, three or four. But if you fear that you cannot treat so many justly, then marry only one."'

Bijan's uncle had four wives and about 30 children, but apart from that the only multiple marriage I knew was that of our neighbours, where the older wife co-operated amicably with the younger in caring for the children of the second marriage.

I did not see women well represented in the workforce. Most who did work were in shops selling women's clothing, occasionally in offices. I did meet a few professional women – teachers and doctors. However, in the whole of politics and the mosque their influence was insignificant, as far as I could ascertain. Ali, Muhammad's successor, is said to have advised that women, being more emotional than men, should have no part in government or war.

One got the feeling that although women were honoured and protected, they were considered in some way 'lightweight', not as responsible as men. In a court of law their testimony carried only half the weight of that of a man. And it was women who took responsibility if men were distracted by their behaviour or dress, or if they raised their eyes or their voices, which could be sexually arousing. They had to keep a low profile, stay in the background, never draw attention to themselves. During menstruation, which was regarded as impure, they did not pray because their prayers would not be received by Allah. It was difficult to avoid seeing women as second-class citizens in such a society.

Everything was different in Bijan's family. They were mostly well-educated people, especially on Mamajan's side, where there was a long tradition of medicine. Her grandfather and father, two of her brothers, two of her children and a son-in-law were, or had been, doctors. Some of them had trained in post-graduate medicine in the West. The whole family had travelled in Europe and the United States, apart from Babajan, who saw no point in it. Their way of life was greatly influenced by those aspects of Western culture that they perceived as valuable.

The married daughters had all chosen their own mates, with only minimal interference from the family. Two had trained professionally, while the third was awaiting the re-opening of the universities. But it was impossible to predict what lay ahead for the emancipation of women under the new regime. I had read that, in some quarters, the movement for women's liberation was seen as a form of colonial domination being forced on Islamic countries by Western influence. I did wonder if this represented the women's view, or that of their male spokesmen.

All these considerations had to be taken into account if I decided to make Iran my home over the long term. I knew that Bijan's family would be watching for signs of pregnancy, but much as I loved and admired them, I decided I could not risk having to leave children behind in their custody if Bijan and I ever needed to part. However, starting a family could be put off for a while, so I decided to stay, and find out where destiny was leading me.

Now that the snows had gone and my chest problems had improved I was able to get out more. My depression had lifted.

I made my wedding dress in anticipation. Having scoured the shops in vain for a fabric that was not synthetic, I chose a chiffon in a soft antique rose. I made it up into a simple but elegant gown with handmade satin roses festooning the draped skirt.

I had been proudly shown many wedding albums by new Iranian brides and knew that the simplicity of my choice would cause raised eyebrows, and probably gossip about the lack of money spent on the outfit. In fact when I told Soraya that I was making my own gown she pulled a face and said, 'You mustn't do that, Anna, it will be ...' and here she hunted for the right word and not finding it, said emphatically, 'zescht!' But I was determined not to be drawn in by the competitive attitude of many of the Iranian women I knew. What I felt in my heart was more important than what I wore on my back. After my recent experience as a 'bride model' I was equally determined not to appear with a startling hairdo and a face so made up as to be almost unrecognisable.

I wanted my wedding to be different, a real heartfelt celebration, a simple but joyful event for all concerned. And so it turned out to be.

No invitations were sent out. Word of mouth was sufficient. This meant we had no idea how many people would come, but that presented no problem to Mamajan and Bijan's sisters who were catering with the help of a most wicked-looking Afghan, one of the thousands of refugees flooding the city. This taciturn character, looking strangely out of place in his turban and baggy pants, sat on Mamajan's kitchen floor for days on end, surrounded by great piles of produce.

The large drawing-room in Mamajan's house was opened up, the dust covers removed, and many more superb carpets brought in and laid in every room from a shed in the back garden.

I was concerned about flowers to decorate the rooms, as no-one seemed to be in charge of this important job. I need not have worried, as many guests arrived with huge floral arrangements in baskets, ready to be set down wherever there was space.

It was a strange feeling preparing myself for the wedding all alone, as I had chosen to do in order to give everyone what I hoped would be a pleasant surprise when I appeared in my home-made gown. How I wished Mother and Lizzie could have been with me, but I had reconciled myself to taking this big step in my life without support from my family when my mother had been unable to get a visa in time to come to Iran for the wedding.

When the finishing touches were all done, and with a dab of my favourite perfume, Bal de Paris, behind each ear, I took up my small sheaf of tuberoses, 'gol Maryam' in Persian, rang the house next door, and went out to the gate to be escorted by Bijan's sisters into the ceremony. And yes, they seemed genuinely delighted with my appearance, turning me around to admire my hair piled up on top, as they had never seen me wear it before, and marvelling at the handmade flowers on the dress and the dainty bouquet I carried.

It all happened just like the wedding I had attended in Tehran during my first few days. The bashful mullah with downcast eyes, the satin sofreh adorned with all the traditional objects, the women gathered near me, calling Bijan to come soon, each time the mullah put the question to me. Finally he did come, handsome as a god in a new cream suit, and sat by my side. Together we signed the register and the mullah left. Now the women crowded in as we exchanged rings, a wide gold band with a single diamond for me, a plain gold band for him. Amid hollering and trilling, they urged me not to take the honeyed spoon, to make him wait, to tease him, to show him I was not one to be walked over – as if he needed to learn that!

I felt the fine rain of sugar on my hair, nose and shoulders, so many smiling faces pressing up close to me, the centre of this strange rite. Was I dreaming? What had all this to do with Anna?

Then, out of the confusion and the commotion came a certainty. This was about trusting Bijan, and putting myself in his hands. This I was content to do; the decision had been made long ago. All this fuss was for others, not for me, and not for him either.

I had been told that Babajan had put aside for me a fund of gold coins, minted in an ancient dynasty and worth very much more than their value in gold. This was my 'bride price' should the marriage ever founder. So all eventualities had been considered.

After the traditional ceremony came the gifting. Few of the guests, other than relatives, brought gifts; if they brought anything it was flowers. But the gifts from the family were all jewellery: necklaces with pendants of precious stones, rings, earrings, bracelets, a very long rope of the most perfect pearls from Mamajan, jewels such as I had never expected to own. I was overcome by the generosity of this family, a quality that had drawn me to Bijan from the beginning.

We then moved in to join the guests, so many I had never seen before, friends of friends who wanted to see the farangi who had stolen Bijan's heart, near neighbours, and of course a great many cousins, aunts, uncles, and young children. I liked the fact that no-one had to be left out because of numbers. I remembered as a child being one of those left out, and how disappointed I felt.

I was a little nervous at the prospect of leading off the dancing with an 'exhibition dance' with Bijan, but Soraya had taught me the movements, and as I adored every kind of dancing and knew I danced well I had nothing to worry about. Everyone was full of praise: for the gracefulness of my dance, for the way I was learning to speak their language, for my appearance, my blonde hair. Zescht indeed! I knew from the warm looks and constant repetitions of 'Bah! Bah!' (an expression of enthusiastic approval) that I had won many hearts.

If some of the men disappeared for a time and came back even more relaxed, I wasn't asking where they went or what they were doing. I knew that some men made their own alcohol in secret, and that opium was sometimes available from the Afghan refugees. However I also knew that Bijan's parents would not countenance anything illegal going on in their home, it was just too dangerous. I relaxed, and joined in the festivities with gusto. We kept the music at a discreet level to avoid the attentions of the pasdaran, but had no visits, for the house is a long way from the street up a private alley. Perhaps even they took a more humane stance where weddings were concerned.

When all the guests had departed except Musa (never my favourite among Bijan's friends), Mitra, Mitra's mother, brother and brother's wife, and a child, I was told that, as they had not booked into a hotel, they would have to stay with us. Several days before the wedding I had cleaned out two vacant rooms in an upper storey and prepared four beds for visiting guests, including two representatives from the New Zealand embassy, and now had to bed down another six people!

OUR WEDDING

I could have reacted with annoyance for their lack of consideration, but Bijan's soft eyes, turned on me so full of love, and appealing for help, melted my heart. So midnight saw me stripped of my finery, dragging mattresses from Mamajan's shed to our apartment and feeling a little like Cinderella.

Delivering the early-morning chai, it was difficult to avoid stepping on the wall-to-wall bodies. Iranians love nothing better than company, so everyone stayed on for two or three days, having a great time, while I managed to play the perfect hostess. Iran had taught me some forbearance already – and I was shaping up as a good Muslim wife!

However, on the strength of that hiccup, a very contrite and grateful Bijan promised to take me to Isfahan for a honeymoon. He would have preferred Venice, but I was quite happy with the city whose name had been familiar to me since early childhood.

The wedding had taken place during the annual two-week holiday called Aid, a time of huge family gatherings and parties leading up to the celebration of Nauroz, or New Year, on 21 March.[14] Each household had on display its traditional six objects symbolising rebirth, just as in our country every house erected its Christmas tree in December. One of these objects was a fish, and I had been a little mystified when, one day just before the holiday time, Babajan arrived at my door offering me a goldfish in a bowl. He had instructed me, with a huge smile, 'No eat! For Aid.'

The culmination of the festivities for Nauroz was a great picnic, on the day called Sizdah-be-Dar, when Iranians went into the country to 'kick out the old year' and welcome the new.

I think all three million Mashadis must have been on the move that day. The main highway was jammed with lorries each holding several families, motorbikes carrying up to five people, cars crammed with happy faces, even some peering out of the open boots. We were held up beside one car that was carrying 21 people according to the driver, surely a feat worthy of the *Guinness Book of Records*. Every vehicle bore its punnet of sprouted wheatgrass attached somewhere on the front. For the first time I saw these people, normally so withdrawn in public and seemingly ground down with cares, now joking and laughing with strangers on the blocked roads, creating a happy cacophony of noise with their hooting horns. No-one in a hurry, no ill tempers.

At every free area on the roadside picnics had already begun. A cloth laid on the ground, a kerosene burner lit, a Persian carpet to sit on, a rope for a child's swing and a chadour hung from a bare branch to give a small measure of privacy. This was formally the first day of spring and the country was beginning to trade its dun colours for a touch of green here and there.

Eventually our cavalcade reached its destination, the orchard of a relative. Carpets were laid on the sparse grass and fires lit to heat the enormous copper pots. We ate and ate, the delicious food washed down with the inevitable Coca-Cola as well as minty abdug, which was always my choice.

Afterwards we girls danced to the rhythm of banged pot lids and clapping. Then, while the older members prayed and rested, some of us headed off for a walk in the foothills of the neighbouring mountains, taking cars as far as we could. Only then did we leave the roadside rubbish behind us, for the Iranians are shocking litter-bugs, a habit that I found strangely at odds with their love of country.

The faintest hint of green tinged the hills, and we could see the beginnings of buds on the thorn bushes at our feet, where soon would be a brief carpet of flowers. We came across a tiny rivulet and followed it up until it was deemed safe to drink the water. Here, miniature irises, grape hyacinths and mint grew among the lush green grass. We plucked long stalks and played 'he loves me, he loves me not' with the children. Everywhere nature was starting to bedeck herself after the harsh winter, and I knew that I was beginning to love this country with all its extremes: extremes of poverty and wealth, extremes of grief and joy, extremes of climate and scenery. And I was happy that I had decided to stay.

CHAPTER 18

THE AMBASSADOR ENTERTAINS

We periodically returned to Tehran, either by air or road, and each time I made a point of visiting my friends at the New Zealand embassy. They had given me a great welcome on my arrival in a somewhat daunting country. The ambassador, Richard Woods, had expressed his concern for me as a New Zealand bride and, as such, a rare bird in that country. Mindful of the possibility of a deteriorating political situation in Iran, he initially obtained Bijan's written permission to fly me out of the country without delay should it be necessary. It was interesting to learn that it was not my permission that was required but that of the male figure who was responsible for me.

On the embassy staff was a delightful Maori woman called Pane, who always made light of the many inconveniences, including power cuts, which affected the air-conditioning and other essential services sometimes for many hours, requiring the staff to stay late to complete their day's work. She had her people's carefree attitude to time and I'm sure this helped her maintain her good spirits.

We sometimes chose to stay with Pane in her rented house in the British embassy compound near the heart of the city rather than with Parvaneh in the suburbs, especially if we were without a car, for public transport from the north of the city was particularly frustrating. Another advantage to staying in the park-like grounds of the British embassy was the large swimming pool. There one could sit out in the evening listening to the thud of ball on racquet from the tennis court nearby and imagine one was in the grounds of a manorial country home in the heart of England, far removed from the stresses of life in Iran.

We were staying with Pane during the month of Ramadan, when all good Muslims take no food or drink, or even medication, between sunrise and sunset. As well as fasting, they are encouraged to read the Koran from end to end. By this sacrifice of their normal lifestyle for 30 days, Shiite Muslims, especially, find a way to recognise the sacrifice of the martyred Ali, murdered at the instigation of one who contested the succession after Muhammad's death. This act of violence established the division that remains to this day between Shiites, who are predominant in Iran, and the Sunnis, who are the majority in the rest of the Islamic world.

I had watched the sweating men unloading trucks, had seen how they hosed their faces, with lips shut tight. I knew that they started work at dawn in order to be able to rest over the hot hours of early afternoon. Here in Tehran, in the overcrowded streets of downtown, it would be even more unpleasant than in Mashad. And here we were sitting by the pool, sipping lemon tea and eating sponge cakes with tiny forks.

How easy it was to blot out the memory of what I had witnessed on the streets, to become a privileged snob for one day.

And then, one evening, we were invited for dinner at the ambassador's home to join others who represented their country in the diplomatic service. To me their life sounded wonderful: moving from capital to capital around the world, enjoying the servants, chauffeured cars, luxurious residences, holidays in exotic locations. Of course I saw only the glamorous face of that lifestyle. I had not considered the isolation from families, or the very difficult climate and conditions that would be encountered in some postings.

It was fun to dress up and be part of this world for one night. Parvaneh lent me her Pièrre Cardin gold and diamond necklace, a most expensive pre-revolution gift from her father, worth far more than even the most beautiful jewellery from my wedding. I felt like a rich woman, and held my head a little higher to show off my borrowed jewels to greater advantage.

We parked our Paykan among several Mercedes and walked up the lit terrace, with its fountain and trailing rock garden, past a pool to the main entrance, where the sleek Pakistani butler, his white gloves stark against his black uniform, waited to welcome us. I paused before entering, to look again over the city beneath us and wonder what sorrows and torments were being unleashed down there; news of a death, an imprisonment, notice of a conscription; a funeral in the family. Life in its chaotic round.

Bijan took my arm and led me inside to the large reception room where 30 or 40 guests were gathered. The female guests glittered. My borrowed jewels could not compete with the flashing of enormous diamonds and emeralds worn by others, especially the wealthy Iranian women, who would outdo women anywhere in the world with the size and value of their jewels.

I had learned that New Zealand's ambassador, Richard Woods, was greatly valued in both Iran and New Zealand for keeping relations between the two countries on a friendly footing. As he and his wife greeted us warmly I was once again grateful for the interest he had shown in my welfare since my arrival in Iran. Now, he took each of us by the arm and led us through the crowd, saying he had a guest of special interest for us to meet.

'Please meet Angela Birjandi, a compatriot of yours, Anna, who has been hiding away by the Caspian Sea for years. We have only just discovered her.'

Before me stood a woman whom I would have judged to have been born here, so well had she taken on the shape and expression of a typical affluent, middle-aged Iranian woman, well bolstered in an elegant gown, heavily made up with an elaborate coiffure, and a little awkward in her very high heels. She told me she had lived here with her Iranian husband for 12 years, had four children, spoke the language fluently and would never leave. This was her home and she loved it.

Coming from the unsophisticated life of a small New Zealand country town, she had adjusted to the twists and turns in the evolution of Iran more successfully than others who belonged here. For me, this was a fascinating encounter and we talked at length comparing notes, particularly about the prejudiced way Iran is viewed from abroad.

At dinner I was seated between the ambassadors from Italy and Spain. The conversation was wide-ranging and exhilarating as we discussed world events and forgot for a time the problems of the country we were in. Mrs Woods had managed to present an excellent meal – for once no rice and khoresh. It was a nostalgic treat, for I often hungered for the sort of food I had been brought up on.

After dinner the cigar trolley came around as coffee and chocolates were served and when a short time later I found my husband, he was puffing on an enormous Havana cigar, the biggest the trolley offered, looking like a young oil tycoon in his well-tailored dinnersuit. This man, who by day sweated in his small factory, hustling for the raw materials he needed and for the money he was owed by the shops he supplied, could have passed as a prince and mixed in the highest society. He was a natural-born aristocrat and gracious human being. I felt so proud of him.

CHAPTER 19

HONEYMOON IN ISFAHAN

I have been looking through the photographs I took that week we spent in Isfahan on our belated honeymoon. How well I recall our first sight of it from the mountain pass that opened up to reveal this oasis in the midst of a desert, this city of trees and roses with its backdrop of rugged mountains.

My father had visited Isfahan before I was born, and sometimes he would set up the projector and show us slides he had taken there: the Imam's mosque with its brilliant mosaic dome shining like a huge turquoise; the palace of Forty Pillars; the great 'maidan' in the centre of the city, a vast open space for polo and other princely sports in bygone times, surrounded by high walls and mosques and palaces, and running up to the imposing portal that led into the main bazaar; the elegant arcaded bridge of Allah Verdi Khan. All this was just a tiny fraction of the glory of this city under its great patron, Shah Abbas, who ruled at the same time as Queen Elizabeth I of England.

The very name Isfahan called up visions of Persia's great past, when it led the civilised world with its culture of glorious architecture and gardens, philosophy and poetry. And here I was at last.

Iran's most famous hotel must be the Shah Abbas. It had been given a new revolutionary name, like every building or street that celebrated Iran's imperial past, but to me it would always be the Shah Abbas. A modern hotel built on the site of an ancient caravanserai, it included one section of the former building restored into a most beautiful annex. I had always imagined that caravanserais were large enclosed stables for keeping the pack animals safe overnight while the traders dossed down in rough dormitories. I had not realised that these buildings were the ancient equivalent of our five-star hotels for the wealthy merchants who travelled with their caravans on Marco Polo's Silk Road to China.

We had chosen the annex, and our suite was palatial, not in terms of size, but in the beauty of the craftsmanship: stalactite ceilings, where the surface was a series of small fans, hand-painted in gold, sky blue, old rose and green; ceramic mosaics on walls and pillars; carpets with patterns outlined by the sheen of silk; wrought-iron screens in sensuous arabesque designs, behind which shone lamps in filigree brass and copper.

The private patio, part of the arcaded facade, looked out on a garden of rose beds, fountains, vine-trailing arches and paths meandering past flowering shrubs. The walled garden had, from ancient times, been called paradaiza, and this was indeed a paradise.

Surrounded by this magic we fell in love all over again, sweeping out the dust and the wedges that had gathered in the corners of our communion: the dust of unshared feelings and the wedges of incomplete understanding.

Without the demands of work, and responsible to no-one except each other, we rebuilt our bridges: the bridge between male and female, logic and emotion, where we often discovered that Bijan was the more emotional and irrational, while I fulfilled the practical, logical role; the bridge between his worldly and my other-worldly concerns; the bridge between the ancient and the modern, Bijan from the ancient civilisation, myself from the infant one, yet he so often the more modern while I found traditional ways richer and more fulfilling; and the biggest bridge, the one we had worked together so long and so hard to build, uniquely ours, the union between East and West, his East, my West, where the greatest challenges to human growth stood in utter opposition, the search for individuality as against the search for belonging.

Most of the tensions in our relationship sprang from these opposing stances. He was always trying to instil in me a sense of responsibility to the family, the greater unit, while I sought space to breathe, to create, to find myself. I knew the dangers of individuality taken too far, the dangers now facing the West, where self-interest reigned. Yet surely the truth lay somewhere in the middle, between blind rule by the clan and total submission to the ego: a willingness to co-operate combined with a sense of personal responsibility. Within the microcosm of our small lives we were facing one of the dilemmas of the world at large: the conflict between tradition and 'progress'.

At times we left the sanctuary of the hotel to explore the city. At Jolfa, a sort of ghetto for Armenian Christians, I revelled in the freedom of being able to walk on the street without coat and headscarf, like the women who lived there free from Islamic restrictions. We stepped into the great cathedral, an island of Christianity in this Muslim world, and learned from a member of the museum staff how the proud and ancient nation of Armenia had simply ceased to exist in 1922 when it became part of the Soviet Union.

From the Ali Qapu palace with its immense open throne room on a high platform, we looked down on the cars racing around the maidan, the largest piazza in the world, a vast rectangular open space surrounded by double-storeyed arcades, with the turquoise dome of the Imam mosque (formerly the Shah's mosque) and the smaller exquisite cream-coloured Lotfollah rising behind.

We slipped our shoes off and entered the stillness of the mosques, empty spaces so different from the clutter of many of the European cathedrals I had visited in the past, with their sculpted figures, effigies, paintings, military banners, bronze plaques and pictorial stained glass. Very beautiful, certainly, but lacking the utter simplicity of great architecture unadorned. In the great mosques of Isfahan I experienced the truth that perfection of proportion has a calming effect on the mind, the great secret of the ancient Greeks. We of the 20th century are not so clever as we like to believe when we create hideous buildings and wonder why they depress us.

We walked the length of the arcaded bridge of the Allah Verdi Khan, the only remaining one of five great bridges. We looked down into the riverbed and saw not water, but debris. There were few tourists to impress these days, and the local authorities obviously had more important priorities than clearing up rubbish.

The palaces of Chehel Sutun (Forty Pillars) and Hasht Behesht (Eight Heavens) were all that remained of the dozens of palatial buildings that once lined the royal route. They were still as poetic as their names. We were amused to see murals showing ambassadors from the court of Queen Elizabeth I in their ruffs and doublet and hose, proof of the extensive diplomatic links that existed 400 years ago. Some restoration of the palaces was taking place, but too often we found the architectural gems from the past unloved and uncared for: the murals defaced wherever they could be reached by grubby or destructive hands; the great frescoes walled off by prudish sensibilities; the gardens unkempt, over-run by lank grasses; and rubbish, rubbish everywhere. Only the mosques and madrasas (religious schools) were maintained in a state of perfection.

So we retreated to the quiet magnificence of the hotel. It was as if this place alone in the whole country had escaped the condemning eye of the komiteh, whose job was to impress on all people that life is a serious business, a matter of survival. Here we did not feel that we were surviving, we felt as if we were living, allowed to live, encouraged to live. I drank in this new freedom with every pore, feeling my head light. Our laughter echoed around the pagoda built in a white marble courtyard lined with poplars, where we sometimes dined; or as we gazed up at the huge chandelier in the foyer, mesmerised by the light filtering in a glitter of colour; or as we descended the curving staircase that fell in a gracious sweep to the marble floor inlaid with a glorious stylised flower; or as I stood on our balcony, drinking in the early-morning scent from a thousand dewy roses, planning another day.

The glorious volcano Mt Damavand, north-east of Tehran. *(Photo: M. Faramarzi)*

At Isfahan we stayed in the converted caravanserai of a grand hotel.

Entering the Sheikh Lutfollah Mosque, Isfahan.

Anna with Chico.

A 'new style' chadour Anna made herself, inspired by European fashions of the past.

Anna among the wildflowers.

Our first view of the 12th century caravanserai on the ancient Silk Road.

On the way to the caravanserai we stopped at a village to ask for directions.

The gateway was locked because the crumbling walls were dangerous.

Anna on her last visit to Te Henga.

CHAPTER 20

IN AND AROUND MASHAD

Early on the first morning after our return from Isfahan I opened the gate to my neighbour, the younger wife. Smiling, she held out to me a large platter heaped with gleaming pale mulberries, topped with a rosebud. The mulberries had come in while we were away and she wanted to welcome us home.

Mulberry trees, known as toot, grew prolifically in Iran. Often the course of a qanat, an underground channel bringing water over the plains from the mountains, could be followed by the row of mulberry trees that were nourished from deep within the ground. They were the joy of the young shepherds, who climbed into their branches for shade and, at this magic time of fruiting, gorged themselves on the soft sweet berries. They had to be eaten almost immediately, or passed on to neighbours, as they soon disintegrated into juice. I never saw them for sale in shops. To enjoy them you needed to pick your own.

In the garden of Bijan's parents stood an ancient shah toot, with its black-red fruit, and for the next few weeks Soraya and I would dress ourselves in old clothes (because the berries make a permanent stain) and climb up a rickety ladder to help ourselves to breakfast every morning. One day we joined the neighbours under their tree to hold a chadour stretched beneath the branches while Bijan climbed up and shook them, causing a hail of fruit.

I made jam and tried to dry the excess on trays in the sun, for dried toot is a popular 'nibble' in Iran. But the sun was not yet hot enough. In the fullness of summer I was to learn just how superb Iranian fruit could be: peaches three times as big as I had ever seen a peach; melons of so many shapes, colours, flavours; and the cherries!

Bijan's friend Joseph had access to his father's orchard on the outskirts of town. It covered several hectares and was surrounded by a very high stone wall, with a massive iron gate. It was a favourite rendezvous for the boys when they wanted to be 'naughty' – to play backgammon or a game of poker, and perhaps try out their latest concoction of fermented raisins.

Water gushed from a large concrete reservoir, flooding the channels that ran between the fruit trees, strawberry bushes crowding to the water's edge. Above the concrete platform next to the reservoir, where we would sit on carpets we had brought with us, cherry trees dipped their branches so low that even from a reclining position you could just reach up and pluck the fruit. The trees were full of nightingales and their song, combined with the sound of rushing water, is forever the music of Iran in my memory.

Zoshk was a small village on the foothills of the ranges near Mashad. It was not a pretty village: all the dwellings were made of the same slate as the mountainside into which it was built. Its greyness was not relieved by bright windowboxes or clambering vines, as one would find in a Swiss village. But at least there was an area flattened out where the village boys could kick a football around.

Unprepossessing as the village was, the surrounding countryside was beautiful. The steep slopes had been zigzagged with water-courses to produce luxuriant growth over the warm season, for wherever there was water in Iran the growth seemed to be phenomenal. Apples, peaches, pears as big as melons, cherries, quinces and apricots, and higher up, almonds and walnuts, were grown here. Valleys studded with Lombardy poplars were fed by torrents of melted snow.

It was necessary to cross one such raging cataract on a very rickety bridge to reach the home and orchard of our friend Akbar. He was an entrepreneurial peasant who had managed to buy a few hectares of the orchard on which he once worked as an employee. He grew exceptionally fine fruit, some of which his wife preserved and made into jam for sale on the roadside. He had also built over the waterway a platform where passers-by could relax for chai, enjoying the almost deafening roar of the water below. There we would sit, six or eight of us, on something resembling a double bed without bed-ends, while Akbar's wife, Mader-i-Ali, hovered and fetched. Their only son was named Ali, hence the mother's title. I never heard her addressed or spoken of in any other way.

Akbar's mother had at times acted as wet-nurse for Bijan, a quite common situation in the Middle East. In spite of the difference in their social standing, always an important factor in Iranian life, the milk-brothers were very close, and we were always welcomed as family and loaded with fruit and preserves to take away with us.

Often we climbed high above the orchards to steep slopes of shale where we slithered and slipped, trying to follow a rocky outcrop wherever we could, to give us hand-holds, while the local boys ran sure-footed as the goats they brought up in summer to graze on the sparse thornbushes. From on high we would look over the broad plain where Mashad lay, ringed by mountains on all sides.

Once, as we descended, we passed an enclosure of mud walls two metres thick, where young lambs and kids were kept penned until they were strong enough to join the flocks on the mountain. The peasants who lived there insisted that we come in for chai, and quickly gathered sticks to heat the heavy brass samovar, while the children were bundled off to put on clean clothes. Cheese, yoghurt and bread were placed before us and we were pressed to eat. A toothless granny sucked happily on a hubble-bubble pipe and invited me to join her, patting the floor beside her. I knew it would be considered an insult to refuse, and rather reluctantly took it up. But I sucked too hard, getting a mouthful of water and causing much mirth, sending the children into hysterical laughter.

When we left a fresh loaf was thrust into my hands. They had no idea who we were or where we came from. I found the generosity of poor people such as these peasants very moving.

In another valley near Mashad we often climbed up to a little circular stone house that had big windows opening over the valley. The owner was long dead, but the locals still spoke of the bulbul (nightingale) who had lived there, a religious hermit, singing his praises out to the inhabitants of the village below.

But my most abiding memory of the orchard at Zoshk was of a day when everyone else went for a scramble up the mountainside, leaving me alone to meditate on a stone platform near the riverbank, encased in rough handwoven blankets. I can still remember the feel of cool air on my skin and sense the blossom petals settling on my hair, the scent of wild lavender and mint, the cleansing sound of water washing down, and the occasional stamping of the goats in their enclosure, accompanied by the hollow echo of their bells. I was alone with the god who recognised my recognition. There was a completeness and I was part of it.

Over summer, Mashad, always a crowded city due to the influx from Afghanistan, became even more hectic with the millions who came on pilgrimage to Haram. I saw many sleeping without even a bed-roll on the pavements near Haram, or in the precincts of the sanctuary itself, where at night the wide courtyards were so covered with sleeping bodies that it was difficult to cross from one side to the other without stepping on someone. There were even tiny babies wrapped like mummies in their swaddling clothes, a habit still practised by the less educated people. I pictured everyone stirring before dawn, rising from the hard ground to go and wash arms, faces and feet in one of the many fountains as a purification rite before the first prayers of the day. Then, after prayer, they would make their way to the huge refectory for the comfort of a warm meal.

Other pilgrims, perhaps those who had arrived by car, chose to camp. We visited a large park on the outskirts of the city where every square metre was occupied by families who had no tents but had strung up chadours from tree to tree to mark their boundaries and perhaps give some shelter from the swirling dust. Each family had set itself up with its carpets, its bed-rolls stacked to one side, its cooking pots and utensils, and its kerosene cooker. In one enclosure a keen housewife was working away on her portable sewing machine, one of her children turning the handle. This, I felt, was carrying domesticity too far!

Of course the time of summer pilgrimage was a great opportunity for the vendors of every kind of food, drink, clothing and tourist memento, and I loved to lose myself in the great swirling, noisy mass of humanity drawn into mutual communion, as if through the power of the great saint whose burial place was the focus of so much hope and devotion.

Once when the weather was good we decided to spend a weekend with Musa and Mitra and some of their relatives who had rented a house at Babolsar on the Caspian Sea. The day after we arrived we all went shopping for food for the weekend, and Mitra bought her little child a bucket and spade for the beach. When we got back to the house he pestered her to take him to the beach, but of course preparing an ambitious meal took precedence, and after lunch it was siesta time until almost dark and little Parvis never got to the beach.

Next day his father put him and Mitra on a bus for the long hot return to Tehran, the child now excitedly believing that they were catching a bus to the beach at last. As he smiled and waved his spade at me from the window of the bus I had to turn my face away quickly. I was really sad because the beach was a short walk from the house where we had been staying, and I had gone several times by myself to sit on a log by the sea and smell the salt air, and even dip my bare feet in when there was no pasdaran surveillance vehicle in sight. But I had not been allowed to take the child with me. He might come to some harm. Someone might kidnap him and I would be unable to prevent it. I was not a mother, but it seemed to me that to bring a child up in such a climate of fear seemed destructive to his development.

But the weekend was saved for me by the chance visit before we left Babolsar to a family who had a pet cat with a litter of kittens. To own a pet in Iran was most unusual. The old biblical idea of man having been created to have dominion over the earth and everything in it was still current thinking. Animals were for sport, to be hunted as portrayed in miniatures, or sources of food or beasts of burden. They were not seen as friends, no. I had often asked peasant boys what name they have given to their donkey, an animal that shared their dwelling as well as their life. I never once found one that had any name at all.

So of course no-one wanted the kittens and they were going to be put down. Remembering our lovely cat Azizam back in New Zealand, I looked at Bijan and he smiled back. And that was how Chico became part of our household.

I really had not anticipated the intense interest in Chico the local wild cats would evince, and a very hostile interest it was. So Chico had to be supervised at all times when outside. But I didn't mind the extra work it involved because he was my baby, he brought me such comfort when he snuggled in my arms, and fun when we played together. I expected Bijan's nephews and nieces to enjoy playing with him too, but they were all terrified, keeping their distance and screaming if he came near. Even the adults were wary, warning me that cats were unhygienic and unpredictable. Everyone thought I was mad. Why not have a baby if I wanted a plaything?

One tomcat was seldom absent now from the top of the wall and one night I woke to see his huge form climbing up the blind that covered our open window. Bijan had borrowed a pellet gun to try to frighten him away, so, Bijan clutching the gun and me with a broom, we let ourselves out silently onto the patio, and then attacked. Round and round the courtyard we chased him, for whenever he tried to jump the high wall he fell back and started off again.

Finally the tomcat made for the trees and hid, motionless. We thought we had lost him when by chance the light of the torch showed up two great yellow eyes staring out at us. Bijan raised the gun and let fly with the pellets, there was a blood-curdling scream, the tree shook as the monster clambered up to the topmost branch, and then we saw his great body soaring through the air to land on the roof of the shed next door. We never saw him again.

Chico's favourite playthings in the garden were two little ibezia silk trees that I had planted when I got news of the death of my favourite uncle back in New Zealand. It was hard to be so far away at such a time with only a most inadequate telephone service to connect me to my loved ones. It was several weeks before I got letters that told me that a few days before his death my uncle had risen from his bed and ridden around his beloved farm, accompanied by his dogs, saying goodbye.

I remembered how each September he would ring me up to say that the kowhai trees were in bloom, and the wild clematis was out, and I would go out to the farm for a day and we would ride the horses round the perimeter of his large property and down steep tracks to get the best views of the hillsides where the gold of the kowhai and the white of the clematis sprayed the green of the bush. And we would return to the homestead with long trails of flowering vine to decorate the mantelpiece.

While Chico stood on his hind legs, boxing the shivery fronds of the silk tree leaves, I sat nearby, remembering New Zealand and sometimes feeling very homesick for the sound of rain on a corrugated iron roof, the crackle of an open fire, the smell of the damp earth after rain at this time of the year. The camellias would be out, and the jonquils. Soon the first cherry blossoms would bring the tuis out of hiding.

Ever since I had stayed in the annex of the hotel in Isfahan I had been pestering Bijan to take me to the ruins of an ancient caravanserai on the Turkmanestan border. There were few of these reminders of the past, for when rail and motor transport became available early in this century, goods ceased to be carried by animal caravans, and most of the caravanserais had been torn down to provide building materials for local peasants. But this particular building was in an extremely isolated area and, according to our informant, in good condition, even after seven or eight centuries.

Bijan borrowed a four-wheel-drive vehicle and a crowd of us, including Soraya and Mehdi, set out early on the three-hour journey. The city was still sleeping but as we left Mashad we saw the knots of Afghanis waiting by the roadside in the hope of being selected for a day's manual work. I asked Bijan how his countrymen felt about these immigrants when the city was already overcrowded, but as Bijan explained, they were Muslims, they were brothers, they had to be made welcome. The modern road bypassed the site of the caravanserai so at a tiny village of two or three simple dwellings we stopped to ask the way and were directed across country, after being pressed to accept a fresh loaf of bread. As we came over the crest of a hill we saw it lying before us on the floor of a green valley splotched with the red of opium poppies. It might have been a film set, so unreal did its walls, corner lookout towers and the impressive portals seem from this distance.

We were disappointed to find the great gate padlocked, but in one place, where the wall was crumbling, we backed up the vehicle and Mehdi, the tallest among us, climbed on its roof and heaved himself up to the top of the wall. Soraya and I, pushed from below and pulled from above, got over easily and the other men followed.

As we picked our way down to ground level through loose bricks Bijan called out to watch for scorpions. This was just the sort of situation they liked! So from then on we kept a sharp lookout for these frightening creatures, which I had thus far never come across.

The caravanserai consisted of a walled quadrangle about the size of a football field, with what would have been a double storey of rooms around the perimeter. The merchandise would have been stored below, and the sleeping quarters above reached by wide flights of steps. The central court, with the remains of a well in the middle, was open to the sky, and here the animals, camels or mules, would have been tethered overnight. We picnicked on the grass that had grown up through the paving, for once without Persian carpets to sit on.

We climbed in the dark up the spiral stairways, stepping warily with scorpions in mind, to the tops of the lookout towers where guards would have watched for armed robbers. Of the two magnificent arched portals, one at each end, one was blind, and obviously only for architectural balance. With just one means of entering, the place was easier to defend. Throughout the caravanserai, in the patterning of brickwork, the graceful curve of a broken arch in an upper gallery, the many fragments of exquisite mosaic in what was left of the ceilings, the towering vaulted arch, or ivan, over the entrance gate, it was obvious that the early builders had been as much concerned with beauty as with function.

When I think of some of the really fine railway stations I have seen in different parts of the world, I wonder whether the ancient caravanserais, with their emphasis on architectural grandeur, did not set a precedent for the buildings that were to become their successors.

CHAPTER 21

HIGH SUMMER

We were now approaching high summer and I began to wonder how I would cope with temperatures such as I had never experienced, except very briefly when travelling through the tropics. Bijan's advice was to avoid getting into light clothes too early. I should learn to tolerate feeling hot without stripping, because my clothing would form an insulation against the heat.

I realised that this was how the peasants and poorer people, without a change of clothes, managed to get through the heat apparently quite comfortably. In the country the young shepherds, still clad in their long trousers and shabby coats, would find a tree, often a mulberry, and climb into its branches to while away the hot hours in the middle of the day, the flocks of sheep and goats gathered in the shade below.

In the spring I had planted a bed of sabsi, five varieties of herbs that we ate every day with our main meal. I watered them well, and was delighted when they pushed through the sandy soil, but not so happy at the wealth of weeds that grew with them. The daily weeding became a chore because of the heat until I reorganised my day. I did my weeding at daybreak and was shortly afterwards on my way to the roundabout to do my shopping.

One morning I neglected the weeding to do another chore that I had been putting off. Like all newlyweds, Bijan and I were eligible for government-funded discounts on certain of the major items needed for setting up a home. We had applied for a gas stove and it had arrived, gleaming in its pristine state. The old gas stove had been carried out into the garden to await cleaning before we advertised it for sale. I could not put off this job any longer, as every time I went into the garden it confronted me. So, armed with rubber gloves, detergent, pot cleaners and a bucket of hot water, I set about the job. As I worked a tune long forgotten came to mind, a sensuous melody with a background of languid arpeggios, music I had danced to as a young girl, called 'In a Persian Garden'. I laughed out loud then, remembering the girl and her dreams. Could she ever have imagined that one day she would be scrubbing a dirty old gas cooker – in a Persian garden?

We soon found sleeping indoors difficult and would lift our mattress onto the patio and lie under a festooning mosquito net. Even so, in the heat of summer the concrete did not cool down until late in the evening, and once the beams of the rising sun slipped over the courtyard wall, a few minutes after I had been woken by the call to prayer, it suddenly became too hot to stay resting. With not many hours of sleep each night an afternoon siesta became a necessity. Work started shortly after dawn, and shops and businesses would stay open until late to compensate for the hours lost during the day.

One day our siesta was broken by the arrival of one of the most beautiful and stately women I have ever seen, with a large bosom and her hair swept back off her face into a small bun. She wore hoops of gold through her ears and her dress was of a gypsy style. Her presence commanded our tiny home, as if she had become its mistress merely by setting foot through the door. She was Babajan's sister, Amejan (paternal aunt), a true Kurd with her large frame and handsome looks. Without formality, she gathered me up in her arms as if I were one of her own children, even though this was our first meeting.

So it was that, on her invitation, we set out a few weeks later for the long drive north to the city of Guchan to visit Amejan and meet her husband, Hassan Agha.

En route we stopped at a small town, for I had been told of a little shop that sold Turkman silver. Everyone in the family apart from Babajan and Bijan despised Turkman silver. I loved it, and found it suited my chosen style of dressing better than formal jewellery. The shop was hardly more than a cupboard, stuffed with goods that hung on every inch of the walls and ceiling.

What a time I had! The wizened old shopkeeper was full of smiles when we left two hours later with our booty: several silver pendants set with agate or coloured glass; some wonderful belts of silver medallions; a set of finely chased teaspoons; an ancient camel bell; two large pieces of striped handwoven wool cloth that I planned to use for upholstery; and two old garments, one an exotic embroidered tunic that I knew would suit me, the other a ceremonial jacket that was certainly not meant to be worn because its sleeves were joined together. But I knew it would make an interesting wall hanging. I left with that feeling of exhilaration that I always experienced after a successful shopping expedition.

Entering the courtyard at Amejan's was like stepping back into the past, a time of graciousness and harmony, far removed from the chaos and sadness of the outside world. The crumbling walls were covered with jasmine and roses in full flower, scenting the air. There were gnarled fruit trees shading the empty pools and dried-up fountains, and stables at the far end of the enclosure, now tumbled down under the weight of rampant creepers. An old brick mansion, its shutters closed like a widow in mourning, stood at one end of the courtyard.

We walked quietly over the worn cobbles, up a flight of stone steps to where french doors stood open. Bijan tapped the glass with his key, sending a piercing yet gentle ring through the house.

As we waited I looked into the dark interior. A fine old carpet covered the entire floor, piles of cushions lined the walls, and the fireplace, wide enough to take big logs, still held the charred remains of an earlier fire. The atmosphere was not fresh, it was dusty and neglected, like the limb of a body surrendered to an incurable disease. It was as if this home, which had held such richness in the past, now contained only the disappointment of the old who have seen too many changes.

A shuffling sound coming from a long way back in the house manifested into a small thin man, whose strong handclasp as he greeted me belied the fragility of his appearance. He spoke a little English even after many years of non-use, but it was easier for us both to speak in Farsi. He seated us outside on cushions on the wide verandah; no chairs, for these people lived as cultured Iranians without the need to adopt European habits.

While Amejan prepared chai for us, Hassan Agha uncoiled a hose and sprayed the courtyard, saying, 'This must do instead of fountains.' Immediately I felt refreshed by a noticeable cooling of the air and settling of the dust.

Then he came to sit beside me and, taking my hand, asked, 'And how, khoshgele, do you like Persia?'

'I love it here, even though the life is often difficult. There is still so much beauty.'

'Beauty! What you see is destruction and decay. Do not think that what you see is the real Persia, it is not!'

He looked deeply into my eyes as he spoke, as if he had an urgent message that had to be delivered and could not rest until it was.

'I love my country. And though I have lived in many places, only this is home to me. But they have destroyed my country, my home. I hate what they have done with Muhammad's words. They have distorted them and imprisoned us with their interpretation. You know I was in jail for three and a half years?'

He released my hand but I still felt his fire and pain. He had been freed only a few weeks earlier, to return to a life now stripped of all its former wealth.

'And as if prison wasn't hard enough for me, it was a big prison and they had a mosque in each corner, so that five times a day from every side I heard the call to prayer. I couldn't get away from it. I am not a Muslim, you see, I follow the old Iranian religion of Zoroaster.'

He paused and seemed to forget we were even there. Then in a whisper, as if to himself, 'And the shots fired in the night, you must have heard them too?'

Yes, I had heard them.

Again he turned on me his tormented eyes. 'It's not so much the economy they are destroying – but yes, I'm afraid they are doing that too – it's the culture. My grandchildren are growing up without any knowledge of their proud history, there is no place for that in education now. It's all religion, and not even our own religion, but one foisted on us by Arab barbarians.

Where can we go in the world now? Iranians are not welcomed any more. Oh yes, I know it was our money they welcomed when we travelled, but at least we were moving in the right direction. The peasants could have emerged from their poverty, there was enough money from our oil, but now ... never!' He spoke like a man whose brain worked too fast, spinning and weaving and burying itself in its tangled threads.

I had met other Iranians who had lost a great deal in the revolution and could not forgive the present regime. I had heard both sides of the story, from those who had rejoiced at the Shah's downfall and those who still longed for the 'good old days'. But most could see at least some of the faults, as well as the benefits, of each system. Not Hassan Agha. I knew it was useless to put another viewpoint to him – Mehdi's viewpoint, for instance.

Amejan arrived with the tray of tea in tiny gold-rimmed glasses, with saucers to match and gold teaspoons. She placed a vase of exquisite roses, yellow blushed with pink, on the carpet between us, and platters of delicate nutty biscuits and fruit, including fresh dates.

'Is he eating your ears?' she asked. I nodded and we all laughed. They could still laugh.

We sat on in the deepening reddish glow of sunset, my favourite time of day, when evening creeps in on silent soothing steps. Earlier in the day I am happy in my solitude, but dusk is a time for sharing.

CHAPTER 22

TAHER ABAD

It was Abbas who suggested our next adventure – Abbas, the hard-working, regular guy who constantly surprised me by coming up with elaborate plans for visiting remote places, and then finding the energy and the gear to make it possible.

This time the plan was to visit and camp in Taher Abad, a village perched high in the fold of the mountains, home to 700 families whose ancestors were forced to find refuge from the invading Mongols under Genghis Khan, a name that I realised stilled caused a thrill of fear among the young children in our family

As Friday is the day of rest and prayer, the men took Thursday off work and we set out, going north towards the border of Turkmanestan. After long hours of driving on rough roads we parked the pickup well off the road beside a river and continued on foot.

A tortuous path followed the winding riverbed, with very little water evident at this time of the year, late summer. Soon we were in a gorge, its sides thick seams of rock standing vertically, broken against the sky like enormous jagged black teeth, often overhanging the path we trod, threatening to fall, frightening life away from beneath.

Wherever I went in Iran, as on this expedition, I saw the evidence of nature labouring on a cosmic scale, creating a violent jumble of mountainous rock slabs, tumbled together and lying at all angles, as if tossed there by some mighty unseen power. To me these awe-inspiring landscapes, the result of eons of convulsions and earthquakes, were also the fearful landscapes of my childhood nightmares, an aspect of the eternity of which I, in some mysterious way, am also a part.

We arrived at the outskirts of the village at dusk and made a simple camp with a hessian barricade in a walled orchard of crusty old fruit trees and ancient grapevines with very thick trunks.

As we sat around the campfire Abbas told us the story of the local inhabitants, originally plain-dwellers who had suffered wave after wave of invasion, for this part of Iran has been a crossroad of armies from north, south, east and west for as long as recorded history. But to escape the unprecedented brutality of the Mongols, these people left their homes and lands to search for a place of safety – high, hidden, where no-one would search them out. And here they had carried on their meagre existence with no quality land, little livestock and few crops. But at least they were safe.

Next morning at dawn two children from the village came shuffling along the path shyly bearing offerings of warm bread, creamy white butter and salty goats' cheese. With wild mint plucked from beside the stream and syrupy sweet tea, breakfast has seldom tasted so good.

The children, a girl and a boy, hovered on the edge of the clearing peering at me. I treated them like wary animals by extending a gesture of friendship, then waiting for a sign of reciprocation. I held out a plate of small biscuits and smiled. They hesitated, but edged closer each time my head was turned away. It was a game of courtship, played unconsciously by these innocents, a testing of trust on which friendship can be built. At last they made their big move and came to sit one either side of me. One more invitation and they helped themselves. I knew I had been accepted.

As the children led us down the dusty path to the village the morning light revealed what had been merely hinted at in the dusk. Mud-slab houses the colour of the earth and textured with the very stone that littered the hills. Naturally camouflaged, they were clustered together so that they overlapped on a high sloping ridge dusted by the sands of the arid valleys below and the bitter winds from the north. A bleak eyrie, lonely in its vigil over the surrounding mountains.

I felt eyes watching and caught a glimpse of faces quickly withdrawn from the high windows. The few women we did see wrapped their fringed shawls more tightly around themselves and passed with lowered eyes.

Did they ever hear news of the outside world? Did they know there had been a revolution, a leader called Khomeyni and now a war? Did they even consider themselves Iranian?

Near the waterhole women squatted washing their clothes. As we approached they gracefully, unhurriedly gathered their possessions and turned away, making room for us. Just one woman stayed and continued her work. Her bold glance of calm curiosity, coupled with her individual choice of action, defined this woman as different. She remained relaxed and unperturbed as I took her photograph.

I sat on a stone wall quite near and we communicated silently, as women. How I wished we could speak. She struck me as one of the most unusual woman I had met in Iran, uncontrolled as she was by the conventions of the tiny world she inhabited. With so little input from people of different experience or vision how did she escape the prison that held the minds of others? She had discovered a freedom in what looked to me like utter bondage. As I left she bade me farewell with a glimmer of a smile and an inclination of her head.

Abbas had discovered that she was the mother of the children, and wife of the headman of the village, who had offered to take us even higher to the mountain orchard and now waited for us with a donkey.

The orchard was a tiny dark green spot high above us on an otherwise colourless mountainscape. I was offered the donkey but chose to walk while the children rode. Initially the track appeared impossibly steep and the weary animal seemed reluctant to begin the ascent, even after a good whack on the rump. I pressed ahead, leaving the men to chatter and smoke.

The sound of voices and the donkey's heavy breathing grew fainter as I strode up the now easier gradient. All was brown and grey, not a blade of green anywhere, only dried and prickly bushes. Suddenly without warning the rocky ledges on one side of the track opened out and I looked down, down, on a great plain littered with small hillocks, layer upon layer of red sculpted shapes moulded by the wind from the north into fantastic forms, with here and there a layer of jagged black rock protruding through the earth. Far beyond, a range of heavy black mountains: the border of Turkmanestan.

For perhaps two hours I climbed and traversed alone, grateful for the solitude, filled with reverence, sensing the spirit of the lonely land with a feeling of awe for all that lay around me.

But then what joy to reach the place where cold clear water seeped out from beneath a rock and sturdy walnut trees dipped their roots into the damp earth. From brilliant scorching sunshine I entered a world of dappled light and cool shadows. There were apple trees too, and grapevines, sprawling blackberry bushes, lavender and mint. A climbing rose had flung and draped itself over the branches of a walnut tree and the tiny pink roses perfumed the cool air.

I sat on a rock and bathed my hot feet in the cold water. I drank, and splashed my face, careless of my clothing. When the rest of the party arrived I felt inarticulate, silenced by the unexpected generosity of nature in the midst of that desolation. I could not find the right words.

As we rested and bathed the children climbed high and pulled off branches heavy with green walnuts. They peeled them deftly, casting off the strong-smelling green husk, which stained their fingers black. The soft brown hugging skin was then peeled off to reveal the naked milky-white nut. A handful rinsed in the spring were then shyly presented to me.

There now came the hollow, sweet sound of bells approaching from the opposite direction from which we had come. A flock of black and brown sheep and goats appeared, followed by a young shepherd walking beside his donkey. The animals made straight for the water, wading in up to their bellies and stirring up the mud. The shepherd was delighted to see us, his first human contact for several days, and broke into an exuberant dialogue with our leader in the local language.

Then, lifting a bag from the back of his donkey, he unplugged a leather cork from the mouth of it and offered it to me. It was explained that this bag, made from the stomach of a sheep and dried to leather-like quality, was filled each day with goats' milk which then, with the warmth of the sun and the motion of the donkey's body, curdled to a thick, somewhat sour kind of yoghurt.

He urged me to drink it through a mouthful of walnuts for a wonderful combination of sweet and tart, cool and warm. Afterwards I felt I had eaten the finest meal of my life – from a gut bag and a walnut tree!

As we prepared to head back down the mountain path in the cool of the late afternoon, I was again invited to mount the donkey and this time accepted gratefully. I felt sorry for the children and asked whether one of them would like to ride with me. Indeed they both would! I now felt sorry for the donkey, but he trudged off seemingly undeterred by his burden, just determined to get home as soon as possible to his nosebag, and soon left the men behind.

The quieting rays of the sun fell on us; the rhythm of the donkey's movement, steady and sure, lulled us; the timeless, spaceless emptiness of the mountains and far-off plains reverberated around us. The silent children began to trust me, to relax their little bodies against mine, to nod their heads with heavy-lidded eyes. I felt their swaying in front of me and behind me, their looseness as they both began to fall asleep. I wrapped one arm forward and one behind me, around their waists, and held them close to me. We became like one bonded, unified creature: the donkey, the children and I, clinging together in an uninviting world.

My mind seemed to expand to fill the silent void around me. It became silent also, a vacuum, emptied, expressionless and impressionless, as I passed into a deeply meditative state.

A great feeling of peace stayed with me as we farewelled our new friends back at the village and set out down the gorge.

Heading back to civilisation, we saw nomads camped not far from the road: shapes and fires, camels kneeling on the gravel chewing their cud, their heads and soft eyes swivelling to watch passers-by, harness and saddles still adorning their bodies, strange and beautiful in the light of a near-full moon.

Abbas drove off the main road towards their camp. We were invited to take tea, brewed in a copper pot over a small fire, and tasting of herbs and smoke. No tents, for the nights were still warm, only carpets laid on the earth and shelters made from camel bags, like low walls around the carpets. The women so graceful and handsome in their reds, oranges, greens and yellows, their long fringed scarves falling from their heads. But shy of us strangers.

I am grateful to Abbas and to so many others who have been willing to share their Iran with me, a country with so many faces, so rich in its culture and history, so fiercely loved by its people.

CHAPTER 23

THE DECISION TO LEAVE IRAN

The heat of summer was fading slowly, thank God. To wake and feel cool air before the dawn was a blessing after days of not knowing where to put myself due to the heat. I had been in Iran a year now, September to September, full circle. But I was still often unsettled. Sometimes I felt 'at home', but the next day I might be wondering what folly had drawn me to this alien place.

I was protected by the tiny world I had built around me. In this refuge I could dream and create another life, alone, with Bijan, and with friends who visited. We found warmth and closeness, trust and intimacy. But even I had to step outside the gates of this tiny haven and face the chaotic world beyond the wall: the world of resigned and weary faces shut down in brooding thoughts; the world of martyrs' funerals, shrines and photographs dominating the streets; this place where everyone was haggling to be able to survive; where the desert incessantly pushed in and layered the city with sand and dust, as if trying to expel the inhabitants, to suffocate them into leaving.

I was also protected from the enormous frustrations of dealing with a bureaucracy that seemed to have gone mad. The one experience of trying to send gifts to the family back in New Zealand was enough. Each time I packed the little boxes and sent them off with Bijan he came back say 'bad news', and each time he went he learned of yet another regulation that applied.

THE DECISION TO LEAVE IRAN

Each parcel must not exceed a certain monetary value. Every article has to be accompanied by its receipt. Where receipts showed more than one article they all had to be grouped together in one package. And so on and so on.

I watched Bijan, ever the optimist, the determined fighter, battling with a world that gave him little reward for his intensive labour. The money he was owed was slow to come, the raw materials he needed were difficult to obtain. Perhaps it was time to move on, to go where there was life and where we could dive in and bathe.

We were both aware of the enormous problems facing mankind: the problems of overpopulation, depletion of resources, pollution, consumerism gone mad, the spread of drugs and the resulting crime and widespread corruption in public as well as private organisations. We also knew, from our reading, that in the early centuries of Islam it had provided in the countries that embraced it a form of enlightened government that had no equal in justice and tolerance, creating a climate in which a great flowering of the arts, philosophy and science had occurred. But for a very long time after that Islam was on the defensive against the Christian world. It had lost its heart and to a degree ossified into a religion of dogma and outward practice, just as Christianity had. Iran under Khomeyni and other great jurists and thinkers was now to demonstrate the renaissance of Islam, and lead it back to its former greatness and power. But we did not believe that adopting standards and a way of life that that been successful many centuries earlier was the answer to today's problems. We could not share Mehdi's optimism about fundamentalist Islam. Perhaps we were wrong. If the world needed a dogmatic religion at all perhaps it needed one as austere and uncompromising as Islam. Certainly many people all over the world seemed to be responding to its call as the answer to the problems facing mankind.

As the poplars began to shed their leaves so too, all the tears for all the tragedy I had witnessed began to loosen themselves from my control. I found myself weeping, weeping – for what? It had all become too strange, this world that my imagination had made bearable for me. Now, through the colours of my fantasies and imaginings, the grey light of a cold reality was appearing. The promise of romance, the mystery of the East, had been buried in the political and economic pressures of a country struggling with its own integrity.

THE SCENT OF ROSEWATER

I was so tired of having to play someone else's game. I longed to rebel, to walk down the street uncovered, to climb onto the table of a dour restaurant and dance, as I had danced in Spain – to break out of the confines that imprisoned me. There was a local woman who was recognised by all, including the pasdaran, as crazy. I would hear people mutter this word, 'divane', when we saw her in the street, gleefully leaping from side to side of the ditches, her hair loose and her legs uncovered for all to see. Sometimes I had a wild desire to throw off my chadour and join her.

I knew why the men drank and the women ate. I understood the restless despair.

Bijan had turned 30 and his passport had been returned from Zahidan, looking as if many muddy feet had trampled over it. At last we were able to consider leaving for a trip – or for good. We both needed to get away. We felt old and worn down.

I had lost my darling Chico. We had left him in Soraya's care when we went to Taher Abad, and returned to find the gate partly open and Chico gone. He had been trying to find a way out into the wide world for a long time and this had been his chance. Still hardly more than a kitten, he had probably been killed and eaten by one of the tomcats.

We booked a return flight to New Zealand via Turkey on the earliest flight available. Early December, before the worst of the winter, we would go.

Meanwhile our home continued to be a haven where the boys, Bijan and his closest friends Arash and Joseph, could let their hair down, sometimes, I'm sorry to say, with the help of a local brew they were offered here and there.

CHAPTER 24

SHIRAZ AND PERSEPOLIS

I did not want to leave Iran without visiting its most famous monument. The ancient Greeks called it Persepolis and this was still the name by which it was known throughout the world, except in Iran where it was Takteh Jamshied, Seat of Kings.

Bijan was unable to leave his work so it was arranged that I would fly to Shiraz with Mamajan and Soraya, who also had never seen Takteh Jamshied.

We flew over the seemingly endless Salt Desert in a south-westerly direction. Looking down from the plane it was easy to see where the Salt Desert began because the network of foot and donkey tracks thinned out and finally disappeared altogether. We were flying over territory totally devoid of life of any sort. I had imagined a desert of salt would be flat, simply a bed of salt left by the draining of the ocean millions of years ago. But the earthquakes for which Iran was noted must have done their work here, pushing the salt up into valleys and ranges and razor-sharp ridges of crystalline whiteness.

As we were approaching Shiraz, Mamajan pointed out the floor of the plain, which was pockmarked with small piles in rows that were beginning to converge, like the spokes of a wheel. These revealed the presence of underground qanats, a unique method since ancient times for channelling the water from the mountains over often very long distances. The mounds were piles of earth marking the access holes, through which the well-diggers got down to clean the channels when they became blocked. The qanats demonstrated the ingenuity and technical ability of engineers in the distant past.

Finally we flew low over a strangely pink lake, landed in Shiraz and stepped out into the warm air and the scent of oleander.

I had my passport with me but it seems that Mamajan and Soraya should have obtained some sort of documentation vouching for their good character before they left home. When we tried to book into a hotel in the centre of town we were refused. Three women without a male escort were suspect. Perhaps Mamajan needed a note from her husband, giving her permission to travel from home, just as the New Zealand ambassador had required written permission from Bijan to get me out of Iran in a hurry, should the political situation turn ugly.

Or perhaps they thought Mamajan was going to put Soraya and me on the streets, to run the risk of being stoned to death for prostitution! Soraya and I thought it was hilarious but Mamajan was furious, and marched us forth from that hotel like a general leading his troops into battle. She refused to discuss the matter with us so I never found out exactly what the problem was.

However, with the help of a friendly taxi driver we found a reasonably pleasant suburban hotel where we were accepted without documents. We proceeded to range through the many empty rooms looking for one with taps and a lavatory that worked, doors that would lock, lights that would turn on, and clean sheets. We had to make a fuss about the sheets but finally settled on a very shabby but moderately clean suite.

It was a vast hotel but we only ever saw one other family in occupation: some Arabs from Syria on holiday. The owner sat with a few cronies in the darkened lobby watching television every day. There was no restaurant in the hotel, no service, in fact no staff that we ever saw. Such was the state of tourism in Iran at that time.

Mamajan had brought a small kerosene primus so that we could avoid eating in restaurants which she, with her extreme Muslim emphasis on cleanliness, considered unhygienic. Food was, therefore, not a memorable aspect of our holiday: bread, fetta cheese, chai, dried yoghurt which had to be reconstituted with much effort, sometimes watermelon, and whatever vegetable we could find to boil up on the primus.

I did not find Shiraz such a beautiful city, though it was the fabled home of roses and nightingales immortalised in the poetry of Hafiz and Sa'di, whose garden tombs were on the outskirts of the city. These tombs, though spectacular, stood in unkempt, weedy grounds littered with rubbish. I wondered if the state of these gardens reflected the attitude of the authorities to the work of these poets, especially when contrasted with the immaculate grounds of the great house, Bagh-i-Eram, formerly a royal palace but now part of the University of Shiraz. There, only the tennis courts were untended. Was this because tennis was traditionally a sport for the wealthy, and now irrelevant? I could only guess at the significance of such clues.

As the streets were deep in mud caused by heavy rain, we bought hideous plastic shoes and spent a lot of time under cover in the bazaar, which was very extensive with its 'main street' and 'side streets'. The shops, which were also workshops, were grouped together in speciality areas. So when you entered the metal workers' part the din made conversation impossible, with hundreds of men banging away on copper, brass and tin. Other areas, like those reserved for cloth dyeing and printing, were more easily identified by the smell or the fumes.

The produce areas were the most colourful, and I was always tempted to plunge my arms into the huge vats of petals from the wild roses that covered the hillsides surrounding Shiraz. I remembered the scent of rosewater that had been sprinkled on the sheets of our honeymoon bed. It is an essential ingredient in many sweets and desserts, and one particular icecream for which Shiraz was famous.

I most enjoyed watching the painters working with the finest brushes made from human or cats' hair on miniature pictures that might take years to complete. One pleasant painter, who was gratified by my interest in his work, told me that the miniature had been brought to Iran from China by the Mongols long before it was refined into a typically Iranian art form.

'Genghis Khan was a monster who left a tower of skulls in Shiraz as a warning to the people, but he also laid the foundations for one of the greatest civilisations in art and architecture,' explained the miniaturist in answer to my question about the history of this genre. I think it was rare for him to find a listener like myself – a European and a tourist. While we talked, Mamajan kept a watchful eye out for pasdaran, who might want to know what, if anything, was my relationship with the man, and why we were talking together.

I was getting desperate to see Persepolis, for our time in Shiraz was coming to an end. But still the rain fell, and Mamajan always said, 'Not today.' Night after night I lay in bed listening to the booming thunder, imagining the lightning darting between those great pillars and illuminating the surrounding desert. That it was so near, and yet out of reach, was a frustration that began to make me moody and unappreciative of what else there was to see and experience in Shiraz.

But on our last day the rain cleared. We hired a taxi for the 40-kilometre drive. Our driver was a young man, well qualified in engineering, but disenchanted with a system that blocked him from a satisfying career due to his lack of interest in Islam and his inability to pass the theological subjects he needed to be eligible for the position he sought. He said that too often the government jobs were going to the 'good Muslims' rather than to those best qualified to do the work, and this accounted for much of the inefficiency evident in government departments.

As we drove along I remembered reading that the land around Persepolis was once very fertile, but deforestation and overgrazing had reduced it to desert. Our driver told us that, in preparation for the celebrations to mark the 2500th anniversary of the founding of the Persian empire, the longest-enduring empire in the history of mankind, a pine forest had been planted in the vicinity so that the tent city for guests would be shaded. This celebration, lavish beyond imagination, had taken place in 1971, when 2500 of the world's wealthiest and most prominent citizens, including every known 'royal' and the cream of Hollywood, had been invited to fly in to join the Shah for the biggest house party in history. How many jumbo jets would have been needed to supply enough alcohol, let alone food?

Why did I feel the prick of tears against my eyelids at the moment we rounded a bend in the road and there they were, the cluster of fingers pointing to the sky? These were all that was left of the hundred columns that had supported the ceiling of the great reception hall before Alexander the Great set fire to it in 330BC, in a fit of either pique or drunkenness, according to which ancient historian you read.

An inconspicuous ticket booth, no guides or guide books, no tourists, just we three on the double stairway, which had been built wide enough to take many horses abreast, leading up to the massive stone platform. Here, two crowned and bearded bull figures guarded the entrance to the courtyard, where 10,000 people could gather in audience before Darius, the king of kings. More wide stairs led in different directions to different palaces, identified by remnants of walls and grand archways. On one wall of the palace of Darius was a long inscription in three of the earliest known written languages. This had been of immeasurable importance to philologists, as through comparison they were helped to interpret the ancient alphabets.

Everywhere there were life-size figures in bas-relief, hundreds and hundreds of them, carved on the walls. There were guards that mounted the stairs in escort beside you, row after row of subject peoples bringing their tribute, leading their animals, servants following the king, holding an umbrella for him as he mounted a staircase, sat on a throne or fought a lion.

These figures were in almost perfect condition after all this time and despite attempts by Arab Muslim invaders to deface them. For, according to Islam, only Allah can create living forms, and no human must try to copy His work. But the task for the iconoclasts must have been either too great: there were evidently too many figures to smash. Fortunately for us they grew tired, and desisted. One theory, however, has it that deep sand covering the ruins protected them from vandalism.

I felt I was surrounded by crowds of people. How much more so must it have felt when they were painted in lifelike colours, some even adorned with gems? However, though no trace of the paint remained the faces were those of real people, each unique.

Over the many centuries, everything that could be carted away from the ruined buildings, from artworks to blocks of stone for peasant dwellings, has been removed. It started with Alexander and his mule trains carrying away the fabulous contents of the Persepolis library to form the basis of his own famous library at Alexandria. Only the massive mythological animal heads littered the floor of the great courtyard, and it was almost surprising that they too had not been rehoused in some museum somewhere.

I wonder why the memory of this great ruin fills me with sadness as well as awe. It may be because it carries such an inescapable message of my own mortality. This place where I now sit and write, in warmth and comfort, looking out at the trees and the mist, will change. Perhaps it will become part of a metropolis, with skyscrapers where my house now stands. It may be overcome by forest, or swept beneath the ocean by a volcanic eruption. Perhaps one day it will be a lifeless nuclear wasteland. But it will change. And the warmth, the good times, the conviviality will be gone, just as the great crowds, the pomp, the significance of it all, have utterly vanished from Persepolis.

Some distance on from Persepolis, halfway up a towering rock wall, four huge cruciform cuttings, with a small entrance hole in the centre of each, dominated the landscape for miles around. Two of them are thought to be the royal burial tombs of Darius and his father, Cyrus the Great. I was particularly interested, because I remembered Cyrus from school days as being greatly respected and loved for his wisdom and kindness. The Old Testament tells the story of his freeing the Jews from their captivity in Babylon under Nebuchadnezzar, and allowing them to return home and rebuild Jerusalem and its temple. He is made to sound like a ruler of great humanity in an era of inhumanity, and I was pleased to be able to pay homage to his memory, while bearing in mind that those who wrote about him at the time were probably well rewarded for their eulogies.

In the end I was sorry to leave Shiraz too, and now hold in my memory so many vignettes from that time: soldiers everywhere on the streets (for it was the nearest big city to the war zone), outstandingly trim in their khaki and high black boots striding purposefully among the desultory crowds; beggars indescribably pitiful, many with empty eye sockets or festering and misshapen limbs, some with limbless bodies making their way on a type of skateboard, others dragging along on slippered hands; scribes and cobblers waiting seated on the pavement to write you a letter or mend your shoes; chadoured women, who would never dare to reveal an ankle, suckling their babies; bikes and motorcycles weaving through the pedestrians on the footpath, where mountains of produce often blocked the way; street vendors touting their wares – drinks, food, cheap cassettes – in raucous voices; carts pulled by donkeys or men; flocks of sheep and goats causing traffic jams; squawking chooks in cages waiting for the chop; old men with faraway looks in their rheumy eyes, smoking hired hubble-bubble pipes; fortune-tellers keeping a shifty eye out for the pasdaran who would descend on them with the wrath of the godly; nomadic women of the Baktiari tribe with henna-dyed hair and hands, walking proudly, swinging their layers of coloured skirts and jangling earrings, guarded jealously by their swaggering menfolk; the green, red and white flags of the revolution fluttering from the buildings and strung across the streets above our heads; the posters – all the revolutionary trappings I had seen in Mashad, Tehran and Isfahan but somehow bigger, bolder, more intrusive here in Shiraz than in those other cities.

And so much noise. Cooing pigeons, vendors' cries, honking horns and revving motors, the whining pleas of beggars, chanted prayers, religious music and messages from the mosques. A dirty, noisy, lively, colourful, absolutely unforgettable city.

How glad I was that Mamajan had understood my need to see Takteh Jamshied and made it possible for me to do so.

CHAPTER 25

'CRIME' AND PUNISHMENT

I remember that night well. It could have been just another of those nights when our home served as a retreat, where tensions could be released, frustration and anger expressed in safety.

Arash was Bijan's best friend. We did not see him as often as we would have liked because his life was weighed down with responsibilities. His father had died when he was still a child, the eldest of seven. As head of the family from an early age, he had supported his widowed mother for years, and was now attempting to launch his younger siblings into independent lives.

There are no government handouts in Iran. It would therefore be impossible for families such as Arash's to stay together but for that most important Muslim ethic of support for the needy. This is considered one of the Five Pillars of Islam. The others are belief in one god; the daily prayers, or namaz; the annual fast of Ramadan, and the hajj to Mecca. Every good Muslim accepts these five actions as his duty.

I was the first woman that Arash had ever really known, apart from his mother and sister. I think with me he felt the first stirrings of longing for a partner, someone to love in a different way. He knew we were soon to leave the country and he expected that we would not return.

That night Arash arrived at our house at about 9pm, just as we were thinking about going to bed. He was very drunk. His close friend Joseph, almost his shadow, was with him. Joseph had also been drinking but not as heavily as Arash. He was concerned for Arash, afraid that he might 'do something stupid'. As if the pair of them had not already been doing something very stupid!

Earlier in the day Arash had been caught up in the long procession carrying martyrs' coffins through the streets to Haram, for the latest putsch into Iraqi territory had cost Iran many casualties. Arash had found himself following the mourners. Not that he personally was involved – the martyrs and their families were all strangers to him – but he had for once been unable to turn his mind away from the waste, the futility of the sacrifice, and the human suffering of those left behind.

He had walked away from Haram in despair and, coming across someone who could supply him with alcohol, had taken it back to his office and started drinking. When Joseph called in at the end of the working day he found Arash black with anger. He wanted to find someone to blame for what was happening to his country. His mood was blasphemous. Joseph hoped that by staying with him, and joining him is a friendly drink, he could lighten the tension. And then he suggested that they should both go to Bijan's. There Arash could swear all he liked – Anna and Bijan would understand.

So they made their way, Joseph driving Arash's car through back streets, successfully avoiding pasdaran roadblocks.

It was difficult to know how to calm Arash. The only safe way was to help him quieten down, and then let him sleep it off. I put on some soothing music but Arash turned up the volume and lurched around the room in a mad desperate dance. Each time I surreptitiously turned it down, fearing a visit by the pasdaran attracted by the noise, he turned it up again.

Finally we got him to sit down and I encouraged him to talk, accepting and allowing whatever tumbled out of his mouth: oaths and curses for the mullahs, for the government, even the prophet himself. Expressions of love for his mother, his country, his younger brothers awaiting call-up. For me and Bijan, his friends who were going to leave him. Murderous threats for Saddam Hussein, for the Shah who had got Iran into such a mess that it needed to be rescued by religious fanatics. On and on. But the tone gradually grew less hysterical and harsh. The tears receded.

Bijan, who had worked a physical 10-hour day mixing chemicals, and faced another within a few hours, went to bed and was soon snoring softly. Joseph slipped off, promising he would walk by back streets and would be safe.

I had hidden Arash's car keys and now indicated the mattress with pillow and rugs I had laid out in the hall area. But Arash, normally as docile as a child, demanded the keys with a determination in his eyes I had never seen before. We were alone facing each other in the night.

'No, Arash, you mustn't go out there. It's too dangerous. Especially it's too dangerous to drive. Stay here with us.'

He stroked my hair. 'Please give me the keys. Don't make me beg.'

I went to Bijan and shook him awake, but he mumbled that we couldn't stop Arash, and turned back to sleep.

Pleading with him did no good. I had never felt so powerless to avert what I strongly sensed was a tragedy just around the corner. I felt tears stinging my eyes as I handed him the keys. He placed his hands on either side of my face and kissed each of my cheeks, then quietly let himself out into the night. The sound of the engine revving in the still night increased my foreboding.

I lay awake for many hours, my body tense and my mind restless, as if my wakeful energy could protect him from harm. I had slept for only an hour or two when I felt Bijan leave the bed in response to the ringing of the telephone. It was Arash's employer, ringing to ask if he had slept here, for he was always at work by 7am. But not today.

I felt a tightness in my chest and panic in my muscles as I waited while Bijan telephoned Arash's mother. He was not there. We didn't know what to do. To call the komiteh might draw attention to him. It was Joseph who came to tell us, within half an hour.

'He was picked up by the guards. Charged with being drunk and blaspheming. He hasn't told them where he was last night but you might get a visit if they find out.'

We were frightened but not for ourselves. We knew we had nothing to hide if they searched the house. But for Arash to be charged with blaspheming, just now, when so many young men were giving their lives for Allah, for all that Islam counted holy – this was perhaps the most serious crime.

It was hard for him to come, three days later, to see us. Especially hard to see me. His head was shaved, his eyes black and bruised, he could not look at me. He allowed Bijan to lift his shirt and look at the swollen wounds, still raw from the wire lash they had struck him with, 80 times. But he would not allow me to see.

It was Joseph who told us that the doctor who had been to see him that morning had spoken of inevitable damage to his spine and internal organs as a result of the flogging.

I knew Arash wanted to cry; the tears were tucked in the corners of his sad eyes. It was as if he had been punished and humiliated for allowing himself to feel. I cried his tears for him.

CHAPTER 26

FAREWELL TO IRAN

A few days before we were to leave Iran, perhaps forever, I wandered around the little place that together we had made so beautiful. In every room there were flowers, some dried ones we had gathered on our walks, and a few last roses from our own garden. I looked at the plaited onions and garlic hanging in the kitchen; the well-stocked fridge and cupboards; my personal belongings in the bedroom, the stack of books that changed each week, my diary, typewriter and sewing machine with some silky stuff half made into a garment, my brushes and cosmetics, the attar of roses and violets and the French perfumes, my clothes hanging beside his in the old Russian wardrobe; on the wall two miniatures that we had so carefully chosen; the silver-framed mirror from our wedding day reflecting our collection of silver and ceramic boxes. Every room was filled with memories – mostly happy, all precious – that I would take with me wherever life led me.

I could not leave without one last visit to Haram, and Bijan felt the same. It was very late on the night before we were to leave Mashad for Tehran. There was still activity in many parts of the huge complex surrounding the shrine, quiet figures reading silently or aloud, bent in prayer or meditation, mullahs conversing in small groups, cleaners up ladders washing the immense chandeliers with rosewater so that the air was charged with sweetness.

But there were few present on the women's side of the tomb, so for once I did not have to battle my way forward towards the grille that protected it. I was able to grasp the bars and stand there for a while without being pushed aside by the normal crush of believers.

As I stood there I thought about this faith that enables the young to go to their death with smiles on their faces, a faith that is causing a world upheaval with its resurgence, and spreading to realms once safely the precinct of other religions.

I had to admire much in this faith, although I could not identify with it, despite having become a nominal Muslim in order to marry Bijan. To me, God could never be a separate being whom I could know only through being instructed about Him by books and teachers. My god had to be one whom I might at some point be able to experience myself. In this way I felt some kinship with the Sufi tradition, the inner dimension of Islam, the heart aspect.

But the Islam I had mostly experienced in Iran was the head aspect, the rules governing outward behaviour. Initially this had seemed almost totally negative, because I was so aware of all the things I must not do. Later, as this imposed behaviour came more easily, I was able to look at the positive aspects of Islam. Although not one person whom I got to know lived anywhere near the impossibly strict and saintly ideal, I still found a great deal to respect in ordinary 'good' Muslims.

I even began to have some understanding of the reasons behind the harsh excesses of the mullahs' regime after the revolution. The younger generation of city Iranians, at least those who had begun to climb out of the pit of poverty, were open to influences that could not be contained. Even if they were too young to remember life before the revolution, they might hear their parents speak about it at times. They had at least occasional access to smuggled tapes of popular Western music, and videos showing a different way of life: miniskirts, dating, dancing, explicit sex, drinking. These objects were passed from hand to hand and listened to or viewed in secret. Likewise, radio and rare magazines were smuggled from the West.

These influences, subtle but powerful, ran through Iranian society and were obstacles in the march back to total submission of a whole nation to the demands of Islam. Khomeyni and his followers believed this to be necessary, to counter the decadence of the West. Any deviation threatened this closed society, where only the mullahs and the ayatollahs had the right to address existential questions. The strictest code of thought and behaviour had to be imposed, otherwise Islam was doomed to drown in the tide of new ideas and ways. Scientific materialism was threatening to engulf not only Iran but the whole world.

Christianity had travelled the same road when its reformers were excommunicated or burned at the stake, when only the clerics had access to the Bible, and their interpretation was the 'only truth'. It took many centuries, many wars and many millions of victims before even a measure of religious tolerance came to Christendom. Looking back at our own history should give some us tolerance for what is happening in Iran.

On our way out from the tomb we stopped at the martyrs' gathering place, a fairly small chapel whose walls and ceilings were plastered over with layer upon layer of photographs of martyrs from the war. On the bare floor, utterly abandoned to sleep like young animals, were about eight teenagers. What were they dreaming, I wondered, and what would be their first thought on waking? Would it be fear, which they would then subdue by an act of will? I cried for them then. Mamajan was not there to rebuke me.

We flew out of Tehran on a bitter December morning in 1984. Having said our goodbyes the night before, we silently left the sleeping house in the darkness of pre-dawn with Ibrahim to drive us to the airport.

As we were getting into the car a chadoured figure appeared out of the gloom, with Koran, tray and water for the ceremony of farewell. Mamajan, dear Mother indeed, the one who had expected so much from me – that I learn the language and adapt to all the stringencies and deprivations gracefully – and taught me so much in the process. But, above all, she had showed me what Islam means in practice. Daunting and forceful though she was, I had come to love her dearly, and it was with sadness that I watched the still figure once more enveloped by darkness as we drove off.

At the airport men and women were separated for the exhaustive body search for gold or gems which, along with carpets and antiques, were not to be taken out of the country. Our luggage was thoroughly searched and my passport inspected. I could go out with only those valuables I had brought in. All my wedding jewellery was left behind, all our possessions except the clothes required for a few weeks, for it was essential that we appear to be going on holiday, not possibly leaving. The travel allowance was so small that we could not afford to stop off en route to New Zealand, except for a few days in Turkey, where an old school friend would put us up.

As we boarded the Turkish airliner a crew member joked with me that I could now remove my chadour. I did so, but for a moment felt very vulnerable under the gaze of strangers, and understood a little of what Persian women must have felt when the chadour was banned. I also felt a pang of disloyalty, as if I was somehow denying the country that had welcomed and sheltered me without reserve.

The Muslims I had come to know had taught me that Islam, for all its strange and, to my way of thinking, often unnecessary conventions, is not a joke, nor a way of life to be despised or mistrusted. In its purity it is based on charity, justice, honour – and tolerance. For Muslims respect the religions of Christians and Jews as 'people of the book' (the Old Testament) like themselves, and honour their descent from Abraham and the patriarchs. This was certainly my experience, as one coming to Iran from a so-called Christian country.

But they fear that the West has little respect for their independence and desire to follow their own religious path, that they are being subjected to a new form of colonialism. Some Muslims, seeing the support of Zionism by the US and the infiltration of Western values, believe they are being subjected to another crusade, which, like the medieval Crusades, is an attempt by the West to weaken and destroy their way of life. Their answer is jihad, the struggle required by all Muslims to uphold the values of Islam, in their own personal lives as well as on the wider world stage.

And the young Palestinians, seeing no justice for their cause, have grown up in anger, an anger that explodes into acts of violence. Is it any wonder then that the Iranian government is not speaking out against the terrorism of organisations such as Hamas, and may in fact be even supporting it? It is tragic that extremist fanatics are bringing fundamentalist Islam into disrepute all over the world, but we need to understand what lies behind those actions, and work towards a resolution, instead of mindlessly condemning.

Surely it's time now for those of us who want peace to seek out what the great religions have in common rather than what divides them. The outward practices and dogma of all the great religions separate them one from the other, causing mistrust that has so often led to war. But if one goes deeper, to find what they all have in common, one finds unity. I like the analogy with the hand. Just as the fingers of the hand are separate, if you follow them down to the root, they are unified in the totality of the hand. I believe that ordinary people like myself have a part to play in rejecting propaganda and refusing to champion one cause against another.

After a relaxing holiday, during which we went through our third marriage ceremony for the benefit of friends and relatives, we settled in Auckland, a city with enough opportunities to satisfy Bijan the entrepreneur. We had to start at the bottom once more, but within a few years had created a promising business.

Bijan and I never went back to Iran together. We learned that life there had become easier over the years, that music was no longer banned and people drove with cassettes blaring, that unmarried couples were safe as long as they had written permission from parents to be together, that the pasdaran had been merged with the police and were no longer feared.

We also heard with much sadness that corruption was becoming widespread again since the death of Khomeyni. Where was Iran headed now? Had all the sacrifices of the revolution been in vain?

In Auckland we became part of an ever-growing family of homesick expatriates who clung to idealised memories that couldn't be tested against reality. The scent of rosewater, a snatch of music, the taste of a certain herb, the sound of a fountain and I too would be back in Mashad, hearing the call to prayer, and the pigeon cooing in my chimney.

EPILOGUE

Anna never returned to Iran with Bijan, but in 1992 she went back there with me. She was diagnosed with breast cancer early in 1991, had a partial mastectomy, and soon after we travelled together to San Diego for holistic treatment at a well-known clinic. She also received a unique form of immunotherapy from a noted doctor who had been barred from practising in the US because his methods contravened the only cancer therapies recognised by the American Medical Association: surgery, radiation, hormone therapy and chemotherapy. Every day for three weeks Harry Alsleben drove us from San Diego over the border into Mexico to a clinic where he was free to continue his practice.

But the form of breast cancer Anna had was extremely aggressive and, despite all efforts, she had to undergo surgery once more back in New Zealand, this time with adjunctive radiation and chemotherapy. But the healthy and most demanding regime she then embarked upon helped to give her one year of superb good health, an unforgettable year into which she packed more experience and joy than many do in a whole lifetime.

I have pictures in my memory of that year, for although she no longer had great need of me, I made my home with her and Bijan so I could attend to the chores, allowing her more free time.

I see her driving very fast in her sleek silver car on the road to Te Henga on Auckland's west coat, where our family had a little old cottage, tucked away behind a headland, a stone's throw from the sea. The sunroof is open and she is singing with Van Morrison, her hair blown back, her slim hand resting lightly on the wheel. Then I see her arrive and, opening the gate in the picket fence, stop to examine almost reverently the latest miracle nature has brought forth in our absence: the first jonquil of early spring, a Christmas lily ready to burst into flower, the swelling buds of the pohutukawa.

I see her sitting at the kauri table painstakingly stitching beads and trim on tiny gifts in exquisite fabric to send to her guru. The fire is crackling, sudden bursts of rain patter on the tin roof, and there is a soughing in the pohutukawa trees, which are bent in the path of the gale and lie along the land after a lifetime of exposure to the wind from the sea.

She loved to walk the hills there, with hat pulled down, warm scarf and gloves. I would have to work hard to keep up with her, puffing behind the striding figure and begging for a halt. On fine days we would clamber down the bank to the little private beach and, with the roar of the tumultuous surf in our ears, practise our yoga and qi gong on the hard sand where twice a day the signs of human activity were erased once more by the tide.

Later in the year she decided to visit Iran to demonstrate to Bijan's family the return of her good health and to ease their concerns. It was still considered unsafe for Bijan to return to his homeland for he had left as for a holiday and could have been seen as a traitor to the cause.

The girl who had arrived there years before from an unknown background, and been accepted by Bijan's family only because she, and only she, was the one he wanted, now returned to a welcome fit for a queen. I was there. I saw it. The outpouring of love was unmistakable, as was the respect for one who had followed her heart willingly into a country torn apart by revolution and a hideous war, had come to understand and appreciate the alien culture more than many who belonged there, and had learned to express herself fluently in the language. The unknown girl had proved herself beyond all expectations.

Returning to New Zealand Anna maintained her physical disciplines in modified form. She cut down her medication and supplements from over 70 pills and capsules a day to those she felt absolutely necessary. Meditation, regular massages, psychotherapy, daily enemas and skin brushing, colonic irrigations, panchakarma oil baths at the Ayurvedic Centre, and a diet of organically grown fruit and vegetables, beans, nuts, seeds and sprouts, vegetable and wheatgrass juices, rejuvelac and herb teas, occasional fish and a very occasional glass of champagne. No meat, sugar, wheat or dairy products.

She practised Egyptian dance, yoga stretching and qi gong. On fine days we would jog to the nearby park for our exercise sessions.

But early in 1993 the cancer made itself felt again, causing searing pain in the spine, increased difficulty in breathing, nausea and disruption of the digestive system. Her oncologist now spoke not of time to be gained but of quality of life. Radiation relieved the pain, her lungs were periodically drained, and chemotherapy killed the newly growing cells, cancerous and non-cancerous alike. But nothing worked to prevent the nausea, and with minimal sustenance she quickly lost weight and strength. We hired a wheelchair to transport her from bed to day-bed, always elegant in her chosen outfit for the day. We took her for walks along little-used paths in local parks and the Auckland Domain, hearing less and less often the tuis' summer song as the weather changed. Sometimes we took the kittens that had been her birthday gift, and they would fly ahead, skidding up trees to show off their prowess.

A week before she died Anna made it known that she wished to discontinue all medication. She asked me to telephone her closest friends to come to say goodbye while there was yet time.

Two days before she died she lost the power of speech, and became comatose for most of the time. Yet I hear still her little quavering voice rising and falling with the tune of the lullabies and songs Lizzie and I sang her as we sat by the bed.

Mamajan, who had come from Iran to be with us, was hosing down the paths, saying that she was cleansing them for the angels that were flying very near now. Bijan was with Anna, holding her hand, when she opened her eyes for the last time. Perhaps it was her choice to die while alone with the man who had brought such richness to her life.

Her friend, the lyric writer Hans Poulsen, wrote a song for her, 'I Carry You in My Heart'.

Anna, I carry you in my heart.

Mary Woodward

CHAPTER NOTES

1. The name Iran derives from the Aryan race which spread, probably from Central Asia, westwards into Northern Europe and south into India and Iran in prehistoric times. Outside Iran, the country was known as Persia up to the accession of Reza Shah early in the present century, when it became recognised by its true name. However, 'Persia', with its romantic connotations, is still used at times for stylistic effect. The name Persia derives from the large area in the south-west known as Fars, which evolved into Pars and gave the name to the Parsees, some of whom emigrated from Iran, taking the Zoroastrian religion to India, where they are today a significant religious minority.

2. The chadour is a semi-circle of fabric, usually black, which falls from the top of the head to the ground, to conceal the body of the wearer. Although Muhammad advised only that women should be modest in their dress, the chadour in various forms has long been a strict requisite for Muslim women in public. Reza Shah, and later his son, the last Shah of Iran, both tried to ban the wearing of the chadour, but for many woman breaking the habit of a lifetime was too difficult and the ban was opposed, especially in the villages.

3. A samovar is a metal container, often ornate, for constantly boiling water to add to the strong tea in the teapot, and keep the teapot warm from its steam. It can be heated by an internal element, or by fire or stove. It is part of every household in Russia and Iran.

4. As a means of suppressing all opposition to the last Shah of Iran, Savak, a huge civilian body of up to 70,000 secret informers, received training in methods of 'intelligence' from the CIA and Israeli personnel. This association helped to fuel widespread anger in Iran against the US and the Zionist regime.

5. Chai, or chi, is the word for tea in many Middle Eastern and Asian countries.

6. The ruhsari is a big scarf used to cover the hair when a woman is not wearing a chadour.

7. After the revolution young men who had been active in overthrowing the Shah formed 'committees' supported by the mosques. They took responsibility for policing the streets in the fight against un-Islamic activities. They had the power to charge, convict and often inflict the penalty on offenders, in accordance with Islamic law. Punishment could include flogging and prison sentences.

8. Agha is the title of respect for a man, roughly equivalent to Mr.

9. Khanum is the title of respect for a woman, roughly equivalent to Mrs.

10. Bazaaris are bazaar traders, Bazaars were always built adjacent to caravanserais and mosques, which were supported financially by the bazaaris. Because of the religious orthodoxy of the bazaaris, it was wise to wear chadour when visiting the bazaar, in order to avoid being upbraided for un-Islamic behaviour and refused service.

11. The word sabsi, meaning green, covers a wide variety of herbs, including mint, several types of parsley, coriander, basil, chives, spring onions and shallots.

12. To Muslims, the Koran is the word of God, received through divine inspiration by the prophet Muhammad. It gives instructions for almost every aspect of life, and tells the story of God's revelation through his prophets, in much the same way as the Old Testament. It is said to lose its divine message in translation. For that reason, Muslims are required to learn to read Arabic, the language of the Koran.

13. A hamam is a public bath-house, a convention that has survived in Muslim countries since Roman times.

14. The introduction of Islam into Iran changed many institutions, but did not succeed in changing the Iranian calendar, and the celebration of the New Year on 21 March, a tradition with its roots in ancient Aryan culture.

ACKNOWLEDGMENTS

Anna died in June 1993 leaving a manuscript unfinished in parts. Her mother, Mary Woodward, realising how much the project had meant to Anna, took on the task of completing the manuscript, using notes, letters and diaries. She now wishes to acknowledge the very practical help she received from Brian Gundy, Jenny Gibbs and Alan Gibbs, and literary advice from Liz Watkinson, Patricia Whitmore, Shirley Dunn and Soraya Millerson.

Thanks to Mr N. Kasraian, 7/47th Street, Seyed Jamalodin, Asad Abadi, Tehran 14735, for his kind permission to reproduce images from his books *Our Homeland Iran* and *Turkmans of Iran*, and to Mr M.T. Faramarzi, 21/66th Street, Seyed Jamalodin, Asad Abadi, Tehran 14369, for the photograph of Mt Damavand from *Travel Guide to Iran*.